T PLAN

PERATING

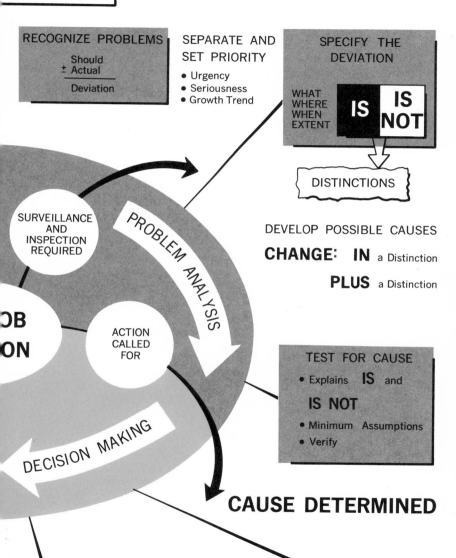

RECOGNIZE PROBLEMS

Should
± Actual
———————
Deviation

SEPARATE AND SET PRIORITY

- Urgency
- Seriousness
- Growth Trend

SPECIFY THE DEVIATION

WHAT
WHERE
WHEN
EXTENT

IS   **IS NOT**

DISTINCTIONS

SURVEILLANCE AND INSPECTION REQUIRED

PROBLEM ANALYSIS

ACTION CALLED FOR

OB
ON

DECISION MAKING

DEVELOP POSSIBLE CAUSES

CHANGE: IN a Distinction

PLUS a Distinction

TEST FOR CAUSE

- Explains **IS** and **IS NOT**
- Minimum Assumptions
- Verify

CAUSE DETERMINED

GENERATE ALTERNATIVE ACTIONS

CLASSIFY OBJECTIVES

MUSTS: Limits

WANTS: Weights

ESTABLISH OBJECTIVES

- Results Produced
- Resources Used

The Rational Manager

PROBLEMS WITH SYSTEM

1. JUMP TO CAUSE

2. FAILURE TO BE PRECISE

3. FAILURE TO CONTRAST
   (IS — IS NOT)

4. FAILURE TO TEST

SYSTEM

STATEMENT OF DEVIATION
   (ALL INFO MUST HANG ON)
      THIS STATEMENT

— SPECIFY — BE PRECISE

IDENTIFY
   WHAT — OBJECT
            OBSERVED

LOCATION
   WHERE — OBSERVED — GEOGRAPHY
            OBJECT — ALL OVER, CERTAIN PLACE
                     ALWAYS THE SAME PLACE

TIME
   WHEN — OBSERVED — ALL THE TIME
                     SPASMODICELLY
                     PERIODICALLY
                     SEASON, MONTH
                     DAY, HR. MINUET

SIZE
   EXTENT
         HOW MUCH
         HOW MANY

```
IS    IS NOT
DISTINCTIONS
CHANGES
```

The Rational Manager

A Systematic Approach to Problem Solving and Decision Making

CHARLES H. KEPNER

BENJAMIN B. TREGOE

Edited with an introduction by PERRIN STRYKER

McGRAW-HILL BOOK COMPANY

New York   San Francisco   Toronto   London   Sydney

RECOGIZE SITUATONS η

1. FINDING CAUSE PA

2. MAKING DECISION DA

3. CONTROLLING DECISION PPA

SEPERATE

PRIORITY

LOCATE (PA - DA - PPA)

THE RATIONAL MANAGER

34175

Third Printing

Acknowledgments

In developing the concepts and procedures described in this book we have had the cooperation and assistance of many individuals and many organizations. We are especially grateful for the help afforded by the clients of Kepner-Tregoe and Associates, including all those managers who, by participating in the training courses, have contributed so directly to the improvement of our teaching efforts as well as providing invaluable evidence from their own experiences. We also deeply appreciate the contributions of those licensed to use these concepts and procedures in training their colleagues. And most particularly we are indebted to our associates, who have not only continually worked to improve the effectiveness of the courses, but have also time and again sharpened and extended the concepts and procedures. Specifically, we are deeply grateful to our first associates, Robert Oliver, John W. Zimmerman, David A. Emery, and George B. Haberkorn, who contributed so much to the sharpening of the original ideas during the early years. We also greatly appreciate the invaluable assistance of the others now on our teaching and development staff: James E. Barrett, John D. Arnold, Robert W. Calland, Tom Earl Smith, William J. Altier, W. Richard

Copp, and Robert B. Miller. And we are indebted to all those staff members, and most especially to Lucile F. Kepner, Eleanor R. Fogg, Julia H. Fulmer, Anna T. Chow, Marion S. Firth, Mary E. Dirac, and Ruth S. Mittelman, who with our editor, Perrin Stryker, have contributed painstakingly to the production of this book.

C.H.K.
B.B.T.

Contents

Introduction

By Perrin Stryker

This book needs no introduction to some 15,000 experienced managers who by 1965 had gone through the training programs developed by Drs. Kepner and Tregoe. It is safe to say that every one of these managers made the same startling discovery that his own private system for handling problems and decisions simply did not work very well and often did not work at all. This is, unfortunately, a discovery that few managers seem to make in the course of their own careers, and they fail to make it largely because the re-education and improvement of their reasoning habits have not been considered necessary.

Yet the cost of unsystematic and irrational thinking by managers is undeniably enormous. If he wants to, any good manager can easily recall from his experience a wide assortment of bungled problems and erroneous decisions. As an executive of a large corporation long honored for its good management once said to me, "The number of undisclosed $10,000 mistakes made in this company every day makes me shudder." However, like others in management, this executive did not think his subordinates could be trained to think more clearly about problems and decisions; he remained inarticulate about his own thought processes and did not seriously question his habits and methods in handling problems and making decisions. This is understandable. It is much easier for a manager to study things like finances, materials, and markets than it is for him to turn his mind upon his own reasoning processes.

Moreover, clear concepts about the reasoning processes used by managers are still scarce. In recent management literature a lot of attention has been paid to the difficulties involved in handling problems and making decisions. (Brief descriptions of some of these studies will be found in the bibliography.) But nearly all the theories and systems proposed seem to be either obscurely complex or obscurely thin and superficial, and they commonly confuse the processes of problem analysis with those of decision making. The arrival of computers and data processing appears to have compounded the confusion. On the one hand, managers are urged to apply computers to their business problems, while, on the other hand, they are frequently reminded that such mechanisms and procedures cannot make their decisions for them. The reminder is essential, for, no matter how many computers he uses, the manager himself still has to know how to reason clearly about problems and their possible solutions.

There is, of course, more involved in being a rational manager than the ability to think through problems and decisions logically and systematically. For one thing, a manager needs good judgment to make good decisions, and this capacity is itself a compound of experience, values, and innate abilities which may dictate courses of action that are not necessarily the products of strictly logical reasoning. Setting objectives and policies similarly involves considerations that may not be reasonable from one or another viewpoint. But the capacity to reason systematically is unquestionably a basic necessity for any manager who hopes to manage well. Successful managers have developed this capacity through experience. But the first chapter of this book shows that even experienced managers are surprisingly inefficient in the ways they go about handling problems and decisions.

It was this inefficiency that attracted the attention of the authors during the 1950s while they were working for the RAND Corporation in California. For several years up to 1958 Kepner, a social psychologist, and Tregoe, a sociologist, had spent most of their time working with advanced systems of defense for the Air Force, and this "ivory tower" occupation eventually got them thinking about the ways people use information in a highly automatic data-processing system. On their own time they studied the effects of automation in industry, and from there it was only a step to the processes of decision making. They soon saw that a great many business decisions were often wretchedly made and extremely costly. They were convinced that there must be some principles and basic techniques that would improve this managerial performance. From their work at RAND they knew that new directions would have to be followed if they were going to develop the underlying concepts of decision making. So they decided to leave their jobs and undertake this research entirely on their own.

The progress of their research is instructive. First, they reviewed the literature on problem solving and decision making, looking for techniques and concepts or principles that might explain the difference between good and poor decision making. They found bits and pieces, but precious little that they considered useful. Then they examined the internal workings of an organization from policy level to accounting procedures, looking at its complete operation. But these business details did not help in finding concepts that could be used in solving problems. Sitting in Tregoe's garage they spent hour after hour trying first one idea or technique and then another, but nothing worked out to their satisfaction. Then one day they completely reversed their attack and decided to start with a problem of a company and work backward through the process of solving it, dissecting the thought process involved at each step.

This engineering approach produced entirely different results. They developed a set of ideas based upon what a manager has to do to solve a problem in real life; then, to help make these ideas visible, they developed a simulation of an imaginary company which they called "APEX." The first problem they posed for research was a series of customer complaints about one style of APEX's screen doors. They chose this problem because Tregoe happened to be looking at his own screen door as they sat in his garage, and they figured that some trouble with a door would be an easy thing to visualize. As they began to think through the details of this screen-door problem, they began to expose some of the common confusions of problem solving; they saw, for instance, that it was no use to advise a manager to "define the problem" before he had even identified which was the most important or urgent problem he had to deal with. Nor was it fruitful for a manager to ask *why* a problem had occurred before he knew exactly *what* it was he had to explain. By such pragmatic thinking they followed through the processes that would be involved in reaching a correct solution, and then backed up their findings with more field research. They spent six months asking managers in a variety of businesses about the steps these managers actually took in solving typical problems and making decisions about them.

This research produced many fresh concepts. While the concepts in existing textbooks were based on one discipline or another, those of Kepner and Tregoe were eclectic and did not fit with even bits and pieces of the established works on problem solving and decision making. For example, they developed the concept of a problem as a deviation from a standard, and the concept of cause as unplanned, unexpected change, and only later learned that Professor Herbert A. Simon was at about the same time independently arriving at similar concepts in his computer research on problem-solving theory. From their analysis of problem solving and decision making, Kepner and Tregoe eventually developed fourteen concepts (summarized in Chapter 3) and then moved on to the process of potential problem analysis which is dealt with in the last chapter of this text. The whole progression took nearly five years to develop to its present stage, and further developments and refinements will undoubtedly follow.

The validity of these concepts and procedures has already

been established in the most convincing way, by practical applications on the job. Some of these applications, described in Chapter 9, demonstrate the flexibility that managers have used in adapting the ideas and techniques to special situations. It is also notable that training in the use of the concepts and procedures has become a regular part of management development in some of the leading United States corporations, including General Motors, Ford, Du Pont, General Electric, Honeywell, and IBM.

Managers themselves will probably find the training methods devised by Kepner and Tregoe and their associates to be as impelling as the concepts. The authors present a full explanation of their teaching methods in the appendix, but I would like to emphasize here that this training provides a kind of experience that managers rarely, if ever, get. In this three-part training method, the first part—study of the concepts—is familiar enough and parallels the kind of vicarious management experience gotten through lectures, discussions, audio-visual and case study methods. The second part—intensive practice of the concepts and procedures in a simulated business situation—is also not entirely new, though in its sophistication and intensity it differs from in-basket techniques, workshops, and role-playing sessions. But the third part of this training—the feedback sessions on actual performance—is not duplicated anywhere else to my knowledge. For these feedback sessions provide the managers with an immediate and detailed critique of their actual performance and show them *how* they went about solving problems and making decisions, *what* was wrong or might be improved, and *how* they can revise their performance. By way of contrast, managers playing business games with computers are in effect simply guessing the computer's philosophy of business and management; they do not learn how they went wrong and specifically how they can improve their decisions—and, of course, such games teach nothing about the analysis of problems.

The research and training methods developed by Kepner

and Tregoe carry certain inevitable and significant implications for anyone interested in the processes of management. Their work clearly shows that problem analysis and decision making are management acts that should be consciously and systematically performed, and if necessary, recorded. The idea that a manager should be conscious of exactly what he is doing while he is managing may not sound revolutionary, but the fact is that such management is seldom found in industry today. The absence of conscious, systematic problem analysis and decision making is not only responsible for inefficiency and waste; it is also responsible, in large part, for the general neglect of two of the most important management functions: the setting of clear objectives, and the setting of clear performance standards for personnel.

Perhaps the most significant implication of the concepts and procedures described in this book is that they anticipate the kind of manager that will be needed in the future. As the authors have pointed out, the continuing increases in technology inevitably mean that managers will know less and less about the skills and knowledge of those they are managing, and will have to depend more and more on their ability to manage the operating techniques of those reporting to them. And in order to manage the way a subordinate handles problems and decisions, a manager has to know how to ask just the right questions. It is precisely with this critical management skill that this book is ultimately concerned. Such skill cannot, of course, be acquired overnight, and one reading of this book will certainly not develop it, but in my judgment there is no better place to start.

CHAPTER 1

Problem Solvers at Work

How do managers solve problems? If managers are asked this, they may respond with some such familiar formula as "First, define the problem," or "Get all the facts of the situation, weigh them, and then make up your mind." But their actual methods of problem solving are often very different. The silent thinking of a manager working alone on a problem is invisible and unreadable, but in a problem-solving conference the joint deliberations of managers on a problem can be easily observed and recorded. In a moment we shall listen to the dialogue of a group of experienced managers as they deal with some company problems. The four managers in this session were working on material specially devised to expose their problem-solving skill. The material is based on actual company records, and each manager had spent about a half hour studying the data for a particular department. All were seriously trying to reach solutions within a time limit, which gave them about an hour after they met in conference. Their conversations are typical of everyday conferences where experienced managers are driving hard to reach the best solutions they can in a hurry.

In this particular conference the general manager has called in his production manager, sales manager, and distribution manager, and he starts off by telling them that "there's one very serious problem here," which is the decline in net income after taxes on some of the company's products. When he has finished giving the figures on this situation, the following dialogue occurs:

DISTRIBUTION MANAGER: Art, if I can add to that, the model C, of course, is bringing in the big profits, and that is one thing where our industry situation is very critical. A key problem, as I see it, is that we're down to less than one-third day's inventory as of this morning, because of the problem of production. I wonder if our real problem isn't what we're going to do about stepping up production, if we can, to give us a chance to build up a little bit of inventory there?

PRODUCTION MANAGER: Just to throw another one out here, Art, it just seems to me from the situation as I see it—Jack indicates we're having complaints from the distributors and we have a problem of low inventory. All this, I think, relates back to our recent change in production methods, and so forth. We had some rejected units, had some sent back, and I think . . .

GENERAL MANAGER: You mean we had some that did get out of here?

DISTRIBUTION MANAGER: Yes, we had twelve units come back, to my knowledge—loose fastenings, the diagonal member bent, and other ones were OK, but in all cases the units were malfunctioning. Now, I think we have to solve this problem, and then hopefully get on to other ones, or else we'll still be subjected to charges of building junk, and complaints, and so forth.

The general manager tries to reassure the distribution manager and sales manager by citing a report that quality control is now back to normal, but then he points to another problem:

GENERAL MANAGER: One bad problem I think you have over there in production, Dick, is the fact that—I wrote a memo to you on this—we heard from industrial relations that Al Hawser, who's chief of quality control, has an ulcer condition, and he never should have come back last week, and he's quite worried about missing time. He's got his young assistant, who's new on the job—he's holding down the fort. Now I think you should possibly check with him and make certain that all quality control procedures are being followed very rigorously, and that we know that he's not, in his enthusiasm, letting something slip out of here.

In this opening exchange we see that these managers are using the word "problem" to mean very different things. The distribution manager, for one, applies the word to three different things: he uses it for something that seems out of line ("less than one-third day's inventory"), then for something he thinks may be causing this trouble ("problem of production"), and then again for action he thinks should be taken ("stepping up production"). This confusion in terms goes unheeded. The production manager promptly calls the low inventory a "problem," while the distribution manager considers that a possible cause of the customer complaints, the "loose fastenings," is "this problem," and the general manager applies the word "problem" to a personnel situation in quality control which he assumes may be the source of trouble.

Altogether in this exchange we see that four trouble spots have been picked out for consideration—the decline in net income on some products, the low inventory, lagging production, and complaints about bad units. Each manager quickly shows a strong tendency to jump to conclusions about the cause of a problem. Note that the distribution manager connects two of the trouble spots (the "low inventory" and the "problem of production"), assuming one is caused by the other. The production manager, for his part, is inclined to attribute two troubles ("low inventory" and the "complaints from the distributors") to the introduction of some new production methods. The general manager, however, sees things still differently: he suggests the complaints were caused by lax quality control procedures. In short, these managers can hardly be described as seeing eye to eye on the situation before them.

Even when the discussion begins to center on one trouble, customer complaints, these managers jump around, going from details (twelve units returned, quality control report), to guessing at causes (low inventory, new production methods, lax quality control) to recommending solutions (stepping up production, checking up on quality control procedures). All these managers are talking about different aspects of the situation. One can strongly suspect that they don't understand it as clearly as they think they do.

But these managers are only just getting started. During the next half hour they discuss the following areas: number of complaints and complaining regions, packaging, shipping, loss of market, trucking, changed suppliers, reject figures, shipping times, engineering, missing the season, production cutbacks, and overtime. The shift from one subject to another generally occurs whenever one manager interrupts another to offer his thinking as to what is causing some trouble, or advice as to how to handle it. The dialogue also shows that the men cannot agree on what a "real" problem is because they continue to mean different things when they refer to a "problem." For instance, at one point after the general manager has reviewed the current figures on the "inventory problem," the following exchange occurs:

DISTRIBUTION MANAGER: Look, Art, are we solving the low inventory problem or are we solving the quality control problem?

GENERAL MANAGER: Both. . . .

DISTRIBUTION MANAGER: I got to get an answer back to these guys!

GENERAL MANAGER: Both, both—the point is that our real problem is to determine whether we are going to ship or not. If we don't ship we're going to be in trouble. Correct, Jack?

DISTRIBUTION MANAGER: And if we ship bad, we're going to be in worse trouble!

Note that the distribution manager now calls both the inventory trouble and the quality trouble "problems," and that the general manager now not only concurs in this but thinks both can be solved at one time, presumably with the same action. Yet the general manager originally introduced the idea that quality control procedures were a possible *cause* of the customer-complaint situation. Before the actual cause has been found, both managers go on to argue over a decision, i.e., what to do about shipping out the units.

As the talk of these four managers moves on, they discuss various other points, and again, as each new subject comes up, the discussion usually veers toward it for a while, then veers away. In the next nine minutes of this conference, the managers discuss units on hand, correcting defective units, complaining regions, shipping, overtime shifts, labor costs, sales breakdown, and production estimates. There is no concentration on any one subject, or any one part of any "problem." Consider the following exchange:

GENERAL MANAGER: I got another thing from industrial relations management where they want some of your space, and I've made a note, and I want you to follow up on this thing and see what this situation is.

PRODUCTION MANAGER: Yeah, well, the fellows out in the shop have . . .

GENERAL MANAGER: Don't bother telling me now.

PRODUCTION MANAGER: . . . have a little space problem out there. There's a little piece over in the corner . . .

GENERAL MANAGER: All right, well, you look into it and let me know, will you? I'll send this to you.

PRODUCTION MANAGER: . . . sounds like all space problems.

GENERAL MANAGER: Now, we're a quality house—our sales are increasing at 10 per cent, which is meeting our goal. Correct?

SALES MANAGER: That's right.

GENERAL MANAGER: I see your letter in here on competitive costs from the field. I don't see that this is a—of course, if our quality isn't straightened out this could become a problem. But I don't see in our big profit line we're higher than our competition. In the East it's not as big a problem as it is in the West. Any comments?

SALES MANAGER: That's right. Pure and simple.

Here the confusion over problems, causes, and decisions is compounded. A request for space is called a "situation" by the general manager, and a "problem" by the production manager. The general manager at first considers that the question of competitive costs in the East "could become a problem," but he then shifts his view and says it *is* a problem, though a smaller one than in the West. In neither case, however, does the general manager look for the cause; instead, he quickly assumes he knows, and he decides what he will do about each problem. He asks the production manager to get more information on the space situation, and he does nothing about the threat of competitive costs, which he minimizes.

Less than two minutes later this conference ended, and in that final period the managers agreed to take one line of action: they decided to make field tests of the product to find out if their suspicions were correct about the cause of one of the troubles they had discussed.

What did this conference accomplish? These managers probed for facts about a lot of things, speculated about some causes, and suggested or made several decisions. However, none of these produced a solution for any problem. Moreover, after nearly an hour of discussing a wide range of topics, these four experienced managers did not succeed in pinning down the cause of a single problem. All their decisions were thus founded on guess and assumption as to what should be corrected.

Why did this happen? What prevented these managers from reaching a clear analysis of at least one of the troubles they discussed? The task they had tackled was not unusually difficult; it involved the kind of detailed and interrelated information that any manager is expected to handle. Then why didn't they handle it more efficiently?

Several reasons showed up very clearly. They did not have a common conception of the job at hand. They did not have a common notion of what a problem is. They did not have an orderly way of approaching the whole task, but rather flew at it piecemeal. They had no way of selecting the most important problems to concentrate on. And they did not have any way of pinning down the cause of any problem they did work on. Their efforts, while valiant, were disorganized and consequently ineffective. They kept shifting from point to point so rapidly that during nearly an hour of conference they talked about some twenty-five different subjects. Information on some

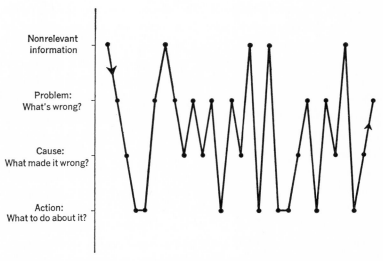

FIGURE 1 A chart of the discussion flow between four managers as quoted in this chapter, showing the sequence in which they dealt with four major categories of information. Their unsystematic shifting from non-relevant data to various problems to possible causes to recommended actions is typical of what happens in management conferences.

of these subjects would undoubtedly be essential for solving any major problem they might have chosen. But they had no way of deciding exactly what such information might be.

The distribution manager illustrated a common series of failings in his opening comments. First he said, "A key problem, as I see it, is that we're down to less than one-third day's inventory as of this morning because of the problem of production." The low inventory clearly concerned him ("situation is very critical"), but he didn't attempt to describe it in detail or determine its importance relative to other problems. Next, he at once attributed the trouble to "the problem of production," and he jumped to this conclusion although he had no real evidence that it was so. Then he immediately proceeded to suggest a decision on the basis of his conclusion, i.e., that the problem could be solved by "stepping up production." A moment later, the general manager committed the same errors when he said that "one bad problem" was the inexperienced young man in quality control and then strongly implied that this man may have been the cause of "letting something slip out of here." Having jumped to this conclusion, the general manager proceeded to make a decision to act on it: he asked the production manager to "make certain all quality control procedures are being followed rigorously," in the belief that this would correct the poor quality problem. And yet there was no evidence that either his conclusion or his decision was warranted. He was simply acting on an assumption, and he apparently did so quite unconsciously.

These and other examples in the dialogue make a point

Low net income
Low inventory
Problem in production
Poor quality product
New production method
Rejected units
Quality control problem
Need for a decision
Need to tighten QC
Space problem
Increasing sales
Competitive costs

FIGURE 2   A chart of the discussion flow between four managers as quoted in this chapter, showing the order in which they dealt with the twelve different subjects they mentioned. Note that there were only two times when the participants stayed on one topic long enough for more than one interchange to take place.

that is unmistakable: managers naturally tend to deal with problems, causes, and decisions without consciously realizing which is which, or where these fit in the process of thinking a problem through. They do not distinguish between what's wrong that needs correcting, what brought the problem about, and what actions to choose to correct it. As a result, they waste a great deal of time and money in their problem solving. They may waste these directly, as these managers did, in discussing a lot of different problems inconclusively; or indirectly, by depriving the organization of the benefits they might produce if they were doing something else, or by tying up other parts of the organization until an effective solution is found.

Most dramatically, managers who are poor problem

solvers can cost a company a lot of money by deciding on an action that proves to be totally irrelevant to the problem. For example, a steel company suddenly acquired a problem when one of its workers was crushed to death by plates under one of the loading cranes. A vice president and five other managers studied the facts on the case, learned that a creeping action of the cranes had been observed, and jumped to the conclusion that this must have been the cause of the accident. So a new electronic control system was ordered installed on all 467 cranes at a cost of more than $3 million. But there were more accidents of the same kind, and they subsequently found the cause to be something else entirely. All the time and money spent on the electronic controls was wasted.

Failures in problem solving trace back to one basic fact: a problem cannot be solved unless its cause is known. A problem is an unwanted effect, something to be corrected or removed. It was brought about by some specific event, or combination of events. To get rid of the effects efficiently, you must know how it came to be. Any decision based on a false cause is going to be ineffective, wastefully expensive, and sometimes downright dangerous.

Here it should be pointed out that every problem has only one real cause. It may be a single event that produces the unwanted effect, or it may be a *combination* of events and conditions operating as if they constituted a single event. The operation of the cause in producing a particular effect is not a matter of probability; it is only our ability as problem solvers to approximate the knowledge of that cause-effect relationship that can be measured in terms of probability. Whether the cause is simple or complex, on the basis of the information ordinarily available to a manager he cannot be absolutely sure of finding it, for he never can be sure he has all the pertinent facts about any problem. But if he follows the procedures outlined in this text he will be sure of finding the relevant possible causes, and one of these will stand out as the most likely cause. This is the cause, an event, or combination of events, that, for all practical purposes, would exactly produce all the facts in the specific description of the problem. (This is the definition of "cause" as used henceforth in this text.) If the manager then wants to go on to have the cause independently verified by actual experiments, he will be as nearly certain as it is possible to be that he has found the cause.

Problem solving is a process that follows a logical sequence. The process begins with identifying the problem, continues with analysis to find the cause, and concludes with decision making. Each stage involves basic concepts. One of these is that a problem is a deviation or an imbalance between what *should* be and what *actually* is happening. And another concept is that this imbalance is caused by a *change* of one kind or another. Until this change is precisely determined, all action to correct the imbalance is merely guesswork. But once the cause of a problem has been found, i.e., that change that actually did produce the imbalance, a sound decision about solving it can be made by the process of choosing between possibilities and selecting the best alternative to get the job done.

These and other concepts about problem solving will be of little value, however, unless a manager really understands them and knows how to apply them on his job. He

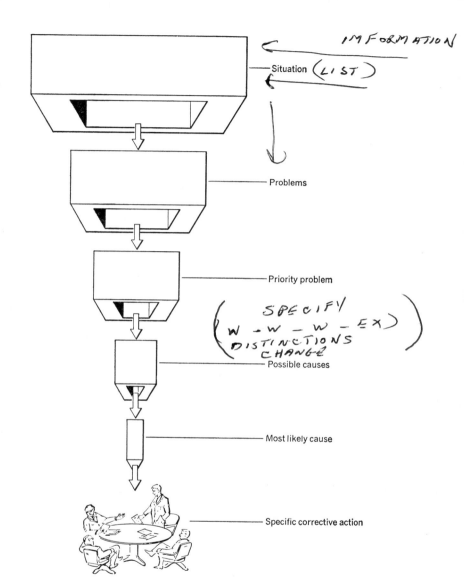

FIGURE 3 Problem analysis is the logical process of narrowing down a body of information during the search for a solution. At each stage, specific information relevant to the problem drops out as the process moves successively from the overall situation to what is wrong within it, then to the most important problem to be treated, then to the possible things that might have caused it to go wrong, and finally to the most likely cause. Locating this cause makes it possible to take a specific, effective action on the problem.

19

P A S T ⟶ *N o w*

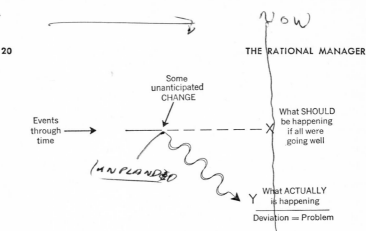

FIGURE 4   Diagram showing the nature of a problem in the course of events. A problem is a deviation between what *should* be happening and what *actually* is happening that is important enough to make someone think the deviation ought to be corrected. An unanticipated change produces this unwanted effect in place of the desired and expected effect. Before this often unknown change occurred, things were going as expected; afterwards, they are out of kilter, off plan, and out of control. Decision making will choose the action necessary to bring things back into line.

has to have some method of efficiently processing all the information about a problem he may be dealing with. He has to sort out the relevant from the irrelevant. Thus, if the four managers quoted above had had a systematic method of processing information, they could have saved practically all the time they spent in shifting from problem to problem, guessing at causes, and proposing decisions about correcting them. They might have selected one or two key problems and developed each of them carefully until they found the cause of each. Then they could have developed specific decisions to correct those particular problems by the most economical and efficient ways.

Instead, as we observed, the managers ended their conference simply with a decision to check up on one possible cause of one problem. They failed to do more mainly because they were not consciously aware of the process they might be following in trying to solve their problems.

But, a manager may ask, so what if I don't recognize what I'm doing while I'm solving problems? What difference does it make as long as I can still come up with workable solutions most of the time? One answer should already be apparent: a manager will almost certainly be more efficient if he is aware of what he is doing during his problem solving. He can assess his own performance and improve it where it is deficient. No manager can ever learn to do better if he does not know how well he is doing in the first place. And raising a manager's batting average on decisions by a few percentage points can mean all the difference between the major leagues and the minors.

But there are other consequences of even more significance. For one thing, unless a manager knows how to go about solving a problem, he can't know for sure whether his subordinates are solving their problems systematically. Though an original trouble may not reappear, the "solution" may still have attacked a false cause, while the real cause was somehow eliminated by other factors or perhaps lies dormant ready to produce the same problem at a later time. What is more important, a manager without a grasp of the problem-solving process cannot tell whether a recommendation by a subordinate is based on clear analysis of a problem or on false assumptions about it. Nor can a manager train his subordinates how to solve problems efficiently if he doesn't know how to do so himself.

The seriousness of these consequences will be most evident to a manager whenever he is transferred to a division or department where the technical information and methods are new to him. There, he often has to manage experts who know far more about the work details than he does. Yet he cannot really manage without knowing how their problems and decisions are being handled. Without some conceptual scheme to tell him what his better-informed subordinates should be doing about these things, what methods of analysis they should be following, he can't begin to monitor their operations or ask the penetrating questions that will improve the net result. He can only trust to his experience and guesswork.

This is not a rare situation in industry today. No manager who is rising in his company can expect to keep up with all the technical information his subordinates down the line are dealing with every day. The higher he goes in management, the further he moves away from the immediate problems his subordinates deal with, and the further he moves away from the knowledge that might help him solve such problems. His kind of technical knowledge soon becomes antiquated and obsolete.

This separation of the manager from the technical knowledge and skills of those he manages has always existed to a degree, but in recent years the separation has increased rapidly as one new technology after another has been developed. The higher a manager climbs in management, the more he resembles the doctor who graduated from medical school so long ago that he no longer understands what modern technologies and discoveries are making possible. Like the doctor, the rising manager becomes more and more dependent on the specialists. Unlike the doctor, however, the manager has the responsibility of guiding and checking the recommendations and actions of these specialists because they are his subordinates. Even for managers with long experience and specialized knowledge of a company's problems this is a very tough job. And often such managers spend a lot of time doing work their subordinates should be doing.

But suppose a manager develops the skill of asking the kind of questions that will tap relevant information about problems? Suppose, for instance, he learns how to probe to determine whether the suspected cause of a problem is likely or not? Or whether the problem he's selected is really important? With such skill it is clear that he would need relatively less experience and specialized knowledge in order to manage the way his subordinates solved problems. In fact, the manager today has no choice. With management growing progressively more complex, and experience more obsolete more rapidly, the manager *must* rely more and more on skillful, rational questioning, and less and less on experience.

CHAPTER 2

Problem Solving under Pressure

No good manager needs to be convinced that problem analysis and decision making are the most important things he does. His success virtually depends on doing these things well. And every manager, consciously or unconsciously, uses some kind of system in doing these things. Few managers, however, recognize all the various phases involved in problem analysis and decision making. Their methods, therefore, are rarely foolproof; they still fall into the traps and errors that block good solutions. Some may argue that they never have enough time on their jobs to apply any systematic method to problems. They say they are forced by urgency to make snap decisions, to rely on intuition. They regard a systematic approach as slow and laborious, not suited to the demands of modern business.

Yet the pitfalls of problem analysis and decision making are almost certain to increase whenever a manager is under pressure—which is usually the case when he is handling very important work. It is precisely at this time, when people are clamoring for action, when he doesn't have all the important information he thinks he needs or all the resources he would like to have, when time is short—it is precisely then that the manager most desperately needs an efficient method for handling problems and decisions. Indeed, any method that doesn't work under such pressures cannot be considered worth trying.

The logic of the manager's job in effect determines the method he should use. He has to know what is wrong before he can make it right. He has to know, specifically, what the problem is, and then proceed to trace down the cause. Not until he has verified the cause can he begin to decide on what is the best action he can take to correct the problem—for "best" implies getting the job done most efficiently. In the sequence from problem to cause to decision, the work of problem analysis closely resembles the search for clues, a kind of "whodunnit." The good manager, like a skilled detective, will spot the relevant information and use it, point by point, to narrow down the search for the real culprit.

Doing this efficiently under pressure is not easy. But it can be done, and the more systematic and logical the method, the faster and more efficiently it will work. A systematic way of doing something is always more efficient and less time-consuming than a disorderly approach that may require doing the same thing over several times in order to get it right. To demonstrate this, we present the following real-life story, which might be called "The Case of the Blackened Filament."

These events took place in a large, well-managed plant making plastic filament for textiles. Though the events occurred in the mid-1930s in the early days of plastics, the

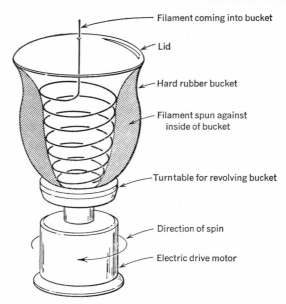

Filament coming into bucket

Lid

Hard rubber bucket

Filament spun against inside of bucket

Turntable for revolving bucket

Direction of spin

Electric drive motor

FIGURE 5   Cross-sectional view of one of the revolving buckets where trouble suddenly appeared in the Case of the Blackened Filament. Plastic filament coming out of the forming machine is whirled into layers against the inside of the bucket.

handling of the problem and the solution is as typical now as it was then. The plant had six huge machines that extruded viscose raw material through tiny nozzles into acid-hardening baths where the viscose streams became plastic strands. Each machine mounted 480 nozzles, and each of the 480 gossamer strands of filament produced was at one point in the process spun into a revolving hard rubber bucket. Centrifugal force of the spinning bucket threw each strand against the side of its bucket and thus built up layers of filament from the outside in toward the center. Every eight hours the cake of filament strands in each bucket had to be emptied, and the process was timed so that the six doffers, the men who tended the buckets, could each empty a bucket on his machine every minute or 480 in an eight-hour shift. This tightly scheduled operation ran like clockwork twenty-four hours a day, with a relief doffer on call should there be any trouble.

Early one morning, trouble came. One of the doffers on the midnight shift emptied bucket No. 232 out on the work table and noticed something strange. Inside the core of the filament cake he saw that the last filament that had come off the machine was dirty black instead of translucent. He didn't stop to wonder about it, however, and went on to empty the next bucket a minute later. Again he saw there was even more blackened plastic in the core of the filament cake, and again he went on to handle the next bucket. When he saw still more black plastic in this one, he yelled for the relief man and turned to the next bucket. Again more blackened plastic. The relief man arrived, took one look and went to search for the foreman. Bucket No. 236 showed up with still more black filament, and the next two buckets showed even more of the stuff.

The doffer now was sure something was radically wrong, but he could only wait for the foreman. He knew what time the trouble had started, for bucket No. 232 was emptied on schedule 232 minutes after he started the shift, or at 3:52 A.M. He kept on emptying buckets and had reached No. 243 when he noticed something different about the plastic filament in the core of this one. There was still plenty of black plastic in the center of the cake but now it was overlain with a few strands of clean, clear filament. And the next bucket showed up with still more of this filament on top of the black. The doffer realized that whatever had been wrong had changed back again and the filament was coming out of the machine and into the buckets clear and translucent as it should. As he went on emptying buckets, he noted that the layer of black plastic was buried deeper and deeper by more and more good clean strands.

When the foreman arrived, the doffer relaxed, for he had done his part well enough. He had recognized the problem at once as one that should be corrected immediately in order to get the plastic filament coming out of the machine clean as it should be. He had called this trouble to the attention of the people who could do something about it. There was very little more he could do now.

The foreman, however, knew that he himself was on the spot. By the time he reached the scene he recognized the problem as obviously a crisis of major proportions. The filament was worth more than a dollar a pound and there was no telling how many pounds would be spoiled. He decided he had better check fast on the five other machines to see if the doffers there had been getting black plastic too. But these doffers reported nothing like that going on. So the foreman at least knew now that the trouble, whatever it was, was limited to the first machine for the time being.

Now the foreman moved into action. Since the filament was hardened in an acid environment it had to move through noncorrosive lead pulleys and ferrules. Perhaps, he speculated, a lead pulley was stuck and the lead was rubbing off onto the filament? Or maybe the hard rubber bucket was somehow discoloring the filament? So he had his men make a visual check of all pulleys and ferrules and of all the bucket lids on the assumption that one of them might be blackening the filament. This inspection of lead fittings and lids took quite a bit of time because he could not shut down the machine (except in case of dire emergencies and he didn't consider this one yet), and the acid environment was enclosed to keep fumes from fouling the air in the factory.

When the inspection was completed the foreman found the pulleys and ferrules for all 480 strands were in good working order. Nothing seemed to be wrong with the buckets either. It had to be something else. Meanwhile each minute another bucket was emptied and another cake of filament turned up contaminated, the dark layer always being a little deeper into the cake as clean plastic continued to come from the machine. The foreman now figured that this problem was beyond him. He went to a phone and called the plant manager who immediately got out of bed, dressed, and headed for the plant.

Note that the foreman took two kinds of action. His first move was useful for it gathered additional important information: he limited the problem to one machine and established that there was no trouble on the other machines. But the second action he took was not useful. He stopped trying to find out more about the problem and jumped into a search for the cause of the trouble. And he came up against a dead end: he couldn't find the cause.

What had the foreman missed? A basic point about the problem: he did not see that it had to do with blackening *many* filaments, not just a few. He had not found out how many strands were involved, although he was aware that more than one filament was affected. He could have described the problem as "many black filaments appearing on machine No. 1 and not on the others," but he didn't. He could have checked the other buckets to learn more about the extent of the problem, but he didn't. In short, he didn't even use the little information he had as well as he might.

When the plant manager arrived, he quickly surveyed the situation. He saw that the black filament had come into the buckets of No. 1 machine and was now being covered by normal filament coming off the machine. Apparently all the filaments had been affected at about the same time in about the same way. There was no trouble yet on the other machines. He reviewed the foreman's action and rejected it at once. The possible cause the foreman had tested was irrelevant to the problem. The cause couldn't be a pulley or a ferrule rubbing lead into the filament since the blackening had affected a number of filaments. It couldn't be rubber coming off one broken lid. Whatever it was, the cause had to be something that would blacken *many* filaments *at the same time.* The foreman had wasted valuable time chasing down an assumed cause.

So the manager at once went after more information. Had all the filaments been affected? He checked all the buckets on machine No. 1 and found that all 480 filaments coming from the machine had been affected by the blackening in some degree. This told him that the cause must be something common to the machine as a whole. What could that be? He immediately suspected two things: the raw material itself or the acid bath. He reasoned that trouble in either of these would affect all filaments coming from the machine. So he also decided to act; he phoned his chief technical man and told him to get dressed and rush down to the plant, and he also ordered the quality control technicians to check both raw material and acid bath for purity. He shortly had the answers: quality control reported that both raw material and the acid bath were pure, clean, and within standards. When the plant manager heard this, he was relieved, but he wanted to find the cause of the blackening to make sure it didn't start happening again.

Where had the plant manager gone wrong? He had been right in gathering more information that told him the cause must be something common in the machines as a whole, but then he did exactly what the foreman had done. He stopped trying to specify dimensions of the problem and jumped into action to check out two possible causes. And his reasoning about the raw material had been erroneous. He overlooked the fact that the raw material came from a common preparation and was therefore the same for all six machines. Had contaminated raw material been the cause of the discoloration, the trouble would have showed up on the other five machines as well as on machine No. 1. Substandard raw material, as a cause, was irrelevant.

Now the technical man arrived and the plant manager briefed him on what had happened. The technical man immediately began to ask a lot of questions. He wanted to know what was wrong, when the trouble first appeared, who saw it, and what was done about it. These were questions that could easily be answered from the information that had been gathered so far. But he also wanted to know more specifically than this what the trouble was. What was the black? Was it some outside coating *on* the plastic, or was it black incorporated *in* the plastic? And what was the black substance itself? Nobody had asked these questions up to this point, and no one had the slightest idea as to the answers.

So the technical man and the plant manager went after more information. They cut open a cake of filament and examined the black strands. The discoloration, they found, was deposited *on* the strand and could be rubbed off. It had, therefore, entered into the process *after* the filament had been formed. The black was taken into the laboratory and within a few minutes was proven to be carbon.

Now the problem was no longer a general one to be described loosely as "some of our filament is black." The problem could be specifically described: "Carbon simultaneously deposited on all 480 filaments of machine No. 1 starting about 3:52 A.M. and lasting for ten minutes." The cause they were searching for was not just *anything* that could conceivably produce blackened filament, but a specific *something* that could coat all 480 filaments on one machine with carbon between 3:52 and 4:03 A.M. without affecting the other five machines. Knowing that there was no source of carbon inside the machine, the technical man said, "The thing we have to explain is the presence of carbon inside machine No. 1 and not the others, and at a precise point of time to coat all 480 filaments at once."

By stating the problem in this specific form, the technical man opened up new avenues of search for cause, and precluded the consideration of a number of inappropriate, nonrelevant, and completely unrewarding possibilities. For the first time, the people responsible for solving the problem knew what it was they were trying to explain. They sat and thought about this for a few minutes. Then the technical man rephrased the problem into a question, "How could carbon get into machine No. 1 and not the others?" The question immediately unlocked information that the foreman had about the machines. He pointed out that each machine had an exhaust fan evacuating fumes from the enclosed acid environment through roof vents, and that the fresh air to replace the exhausted fumes came into the machine through a large duct with an air intake at the rear of the building. Each machine had its own exhaust system and fresh-air intake. "Stuff could come into the machine through the intake of one air-exhaust system," the foreman said, "and it wouldn't affect the other machines."

The technical man then asked a more specific question: "What is a local source of airborne carbon?" Several people at once suggested the source could be the coal-burning boiler house, and the stationary engineer was summoned and queried. When did he blow the stacks on his boiler? "At midnight, the same as I always do," the engineer replied. This didn't check out with the time of the trouble. Besides, the technical man reasoned, if the soot from the boiler tubes had drifted across the plant building then probably more than one machine would have sucked it in. So one more possible cause was eliminated.

Now the technical man sharpened up his questioning. "What we need," he reminded them, "is a small local source of carbon that could affect one machine and not the others. How could soot get into one air intake and not the others?" The plant manager thought a minute and then said, "Something like a cloud of smoke from a locomotive. . . ." He paused, then immediately asked, "Was there a switch engine in the yard last night?" Now they summoned the yard man who answered a series of quick questions. Yes, a coal-burning switcher had come into the yard with a string of box cars. Yes, it had been about 3:30 A.M. Yes, after spotting the cars the switcher had stopped on the track behind the plant building, immediately behind machine No. 1 and about under the air intake, while the crew came inside for a cup of coffee. What time was that? About 3:45 A.M. maybe a little later. There was a light breeze that night that would have carried the smoke toward the air intake.

Everything checked out against their specific description of the problem. They had found the cause of the black on the plastic. The air intake had sucked in the greasy, black smoke from the stack of the coal-burning switch engine. The soot had settled on the filaments as they rose from the acid bath and moved into the buckets. When the crew had finished coffee ten minutes later, around 4 A.M., the engine had moved away, the black carbon being deposited on the filament had vanished, and the plastic again came from the machine clear and translucent as it should be.

Technically, this was a case of successful problem analysis because they ultimately found the cause of the problem. But it was certainly not a good example of efficient information handling. The people involved went up a number of blind alleys in their investigation. They came perilously close, a number of times, to accepting a wrong conclusion about the problem and going off into completely non-relevant action. Their major mistakes were these:

1. They did a poor job of getting the information out

about the situation. Vital information came out by bits and pieces. They did not consciously sit down to explore what was known and what was not known about the trouble. They did not try to organize the available information into a coherent, consistent, and specific picture of what was going on. They proved pretty well by their actions that an attempt to solve a problem before vital information has been dug out is doomed to failure.

2. They did not attempt to state the problem specifically. They did not find out the exact dimensions of the problem, i.e., that it was carbon deposited on the filament in one machine at a certain point in time. They dealt with the problem simply as "black filament." Yet, except by lucky accident, they never could have found the cause until the black was specified as carbon, not just something dark.

3. They looked too quickly for possible causes. They were trying to explain the presence of the black without knowing what the black was. They wasted a good deal of time exploring and testing out speculations about cause that could have no possible relationship to the problem. Therefore, three of the four tries they made at finding the cause—checking ferrules and pulleys, buckets, and raw materials—produced no useful information.

It was the chief technical man who finally led them to the cause. How? By asking questions about the problem that pulled out relevant, factual information. It took only fifteen questions to get out the vital information, locate the cause, and check it out. Actually, the necessary information was drawn out by these basic questions: What is wrong and what does it affect? Where does it occur? When

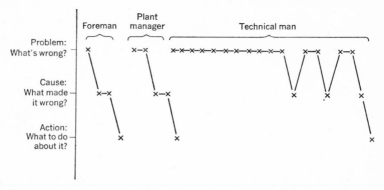

FIGURE 6   A chart of the kinds of questions asked by three people in the Case of the Blackened Filament. Note how the technical man asked a lot of questions about the problem first, before asking about cause, and then twice returned to the problem for more information. When he finally determined the cause, he tested this against the problem before he proceeded to corrective action. Compare the pattern of his systematic approach against the hit-or-miss attack in the dialogue charted in Figure 1 on page 14.

does it occur? How big is it? The answers framed in the dimensions of the problem and specified it exactly. Once that was done, the men moved rapidly and efficiently to a correct conclusion. They found that the real culprit was the coal smoke from the switch engine.

Unfortunately, these problem analyzers did not fare so well as decision makers. The possibility that carbon or some other contaminant might come into the machine at some future time worried them. It had happened once and it might happen again. Within a few days, they decided to install oil-bath air filters on each of the air intakes. They were aware that a very slight oil film would be deposited on the filament but felt that this would be no problem since the plastic would all be spray-washed with solvent and rewound before shipment to the customer. Within three weeks, however, there was such a coating of oil on everything else that the buckets became slippery. It was no longer possible for the doffers to empty one each minute to keep up with the machine. They had to reorganize the whole doffer operation which cost many times more than did the filtration system. Then, a short time later, they had to replace the new oil-bath filters with another type altogether. In short, the corrective action they settled on caused new problems in turn, more costly in the long run than the initial problem they set out to solve.

They made four big mistakes in their decision making, and three of these paralleled the errors they had made in problem analysis. First, they failed to specify their purpose in making a decision, just as they had failed to specify the problem at the outset. Because they didn't specify in advance what they wanted the decision to accomplish, they could not be sure they were choosing the best action to achieve that end. Second, they plunged into action to buy the oil-bath filtration system without considering other relevant alternatives, just as they had plunged into action to test out possible causes which had no connection with the problem. Third, they made poor use of the information available to them, just as they had in their problem analysis. They never asked what the probability was that another switch engine would ever park exactly under an air intake, particularly if they took precautions to prevent it. Fourth, they failed to look at the consequences of their action and to assess its future costs. They considered the effect of the oil film on the filament only, not on other things essential to the operation. In the long run, the effects of their decision cost them many times more than the loss—probably less than $12,000—from the problem they set out to correct.

The Case of the Blackened Filament contains a lot of lessons. Certainly one big lesson is that a manager without a systematic approach to problem solving and decision making is not likely to produce the best results. He will waste time chasing up blind alleys after impossible causes. He will miss and skip over vital information, be forced to go back again and again to the same questions in order to get useful answers. And he may come to the wrong conclusion entirely.

But an equally big lesson is that the errors these managers made in this case were avoidable. They occurred because the managers did not appear to know how to go about consciously handling the information. They lacked two things: first, a body of concepts, a clear picture of what they were trying to do and where they were trying to go in analyzing the problem and making the decision; and second, they needed an orderly and systematic way of progressing along the problem-cause-decision sequence. These things we will discuss in the next chapter.

CHAPTER **3**

The Concepts and the Methods

How can the manager improve his performance in analyzing problems? The key to the answer lies in the fundamental fact that the raw material of management is information. This is all that any manager has to work with —information about the world around him, about his organization and its plans, about the performance of that segment of the organization where he is responsible for carrying out those plans, about people and things and conditions. He has to know what information he has about any problem, what information he doesn't have and how he can get it, and how he can use all the information he has to the best advantage in getting the problem solved. He must be as perceptive in recognizing, before the fact, what information will be relevant and important and what will not as he is in recognizing, with the benefit of hindsight, the obvious relevance and importance of certain information.

Managers are supposed to learn such skills naturally as a by-product of their experience in business. The general assumption is that because everyone deals with information every day in his own line of activity, everyone should therefore know equally well how to use information efficiently. This, of course, is simply not true. Some people are far more skilled in using information than others, and some receive more instruction in this than others. For example, the scientist and the doctor go through elaborate courses of training in order to learn objective methods of using information in the solution of technical problems. Here the cost of handling information poorly can be deadly, and though their methods may not be consciously systematic, their predecessors have established safe routines. The manager, however, who must constantly analyze problems and make decisions, and who, therefore, perhaps more than anyone else needs efficient ways of working with information, has been left to shift for himself. The result is usually what we observed in the preceding chapter—a hit-and-miss approach based on a mixture of experience and guesswork.

What a manager needs for effective problem analysis is an orderly system for processing information, a system in which certain steps follow others in a fixed order. To apply logical methods of analysis, the manager must understand the distinction between problem analysis and decision making, and he must also have a grasp of the concepts underlying each of these processes. Two of the main concepts of problem analysis have already been mentioned: one is that every problem is a deviation from some standard of expected performance, and the other is that a change of some kind is always the cause of a problem. Concepts such as these provide the manager with a roadmap of what he is trying to do, where he is trying to go in analyzing problems and making decisions.

Concepts alone, however, are not enough. A manager should also be conscious of an orderly and efficient method of progressing along the paths outlined by the roadmap in order to get the job done. Based on the concepts, the method will show him *what* to do and *when* to do it, *what* information he should use and *how* he should use it. By way of contrast, the familiar step-by-step procedures commonly recommended for managers may say that a manager should "get all the facts" and "define the problem." This is all very well, but very little is ever said as to *how* he does this, and *what* he does with information once he has it.

A manager who understands the concepts underlying problem analysis and has a systematic method for going through the process gains these important advantages:

1. He knows where he (or a subordinate) is at any time in the process. Until he knows where he is in the process, he can't tell what information is relevant and what is not.

2. Because this process is understood and visible to him, the manager has a framework to guide him in the handling of information to produce a correct solution.

With these advantages, the manager can see his own errors and improve his performance in problem analysis; and, what is equally important, he can identify the errors of his subordinates and develop their competence in problem analysis.

The authors have identified, through observing the tactics of practicing managers, seven basic concepts in problem analysis and seven in decision making. Together these fourteen concepts comprise a two-part cycle, one half covering problem analysis and the other half decision making. The manager who grasps them will not make the common error of confusing problem analysis (getting to the cause) with decision making (choosing what to do about it). Furthermore, he is not likely to jump to conclusions about the cause of a problem.

This text is confined to problem analysis primarily, but the concepts underlying both problem analysis and decision making are so interrelated that an understanding of the whole sequence is necessary for any manager desiring to use information efficiently. The concepts themselves are not complicated; they are simple and rational.

To illustrate and describe these concepts, let us go back for a moment to the Case of the Blackened Filament. Briefly, the trouble to be explained was the sudden, unwanted appearance of blackened filament. This was the effect of something else that had occurred at the time and was unknown to the managers involved. After considerable analysis, these managers determined the cause to be the coal smoke from a switch engine parked under the air intake serving one of the six extruding machines. If we now start with this explanation of the problem and trace the sequence of events back to the beginning of the trouble, we can see the logical steps of relating cause to effect.

First there was coal smoke from a switch engine parked near the building where a breeze carried its smoke to the air intake for machine No. 1. The advent of carbon in the form of coal smoke in this intake was a change from conditions that existed previously. It was only one of many changes occurring at that time, but it was the one particular change capable of producing the specific effect of carbon-blackened filament only in machine No. 1 and during a definite interval. Now this particular change had achieved its specific effect through features, mechanisms, and conditions that were distinctive of the problem. One of these distinctions was in the carbon itself. What was distinctive of this carbon? Carbon was not used inside the plant so it must have come from an outside source. A second distinction was in machine No. 1. What features or mechanism or conditions were distinctive of this machine? There was clearly one: it had its own air intake that was separately located in space for that one machine; all the intakes of the five other machines were located elsewhere in space. And a third distinction was in the exact period of time when the trouble occurred, i.e., between 3:52 and 4:03 A.M. What was distinctive of this period? It was just during this period that a switch engine had been parked under the air intake of machine No. 1. All together, these distinctions clearly characterized the specific effect produced by the change that had caused the problem. The whole sequence was: change (coal smoke) operated through three distinctive features, mechanisms, and conditions (carbon from outside the plant, a specific air intake, a parked switch engine) to cause a specific effect (blackened filament on machine No. 1 and not on five others).

Now let us look at this process in its original order. To begin with, these managers recognized the problem at once because they each had a definite idea as to what kind of filament should be coming out of the machines and they knew blackened filament was definitely out of order. That is, they had standards of performance that alerted them to whatever went wrong in production. After several false starts on the problem, the technical manager arrived and determined, first, the dimensions of the problem—what it was, when and where it occurred, and how big it was. Next the managers probed into these facts for clues and eventually found the distinctions noted above—the carbon from an outside source, the location of a separate air intake for machine No. 1, and the presence of a switch engine parked under that air intake just when the filament was being blackened. Then the managers considered the changes that had occurred that night and finally determined that only one particular change (coal smoke from the switch engine) was unmistakably connected with the distinctions they had found. They concluded that this one change alone could have produced the specific effect they had recognized as the problem.

Thus, by a series of steps, these managers arrived at the cause of their problem. These steps are stated formally in the seven basic concepts of problem analysis that follow:

X   1. *The problem analyzer has an expected standard of performance, a "should" against which to compare actual performance.* Thus the doffer, foreman, plant manager, and technical man all knew that the plastic should come out in clear translucent filament. The first action required in problem analysis is for the manager to recognize problem areas. He does this by surveying the situation within his responsibility, comparing what is actually going on with what he believes should be going on.

2. *A problem is a deviation from a standard of performance.* The appearance of the blackened filament, a dramatic deviation from the expected clear production, was

the problem to be analyzed in the filament case. Usually a manager has to select one out of several problems to work on, and he does this by <u>establishing priorities of urgency, seriousness, and potential for growth.</u>

3. *A deviation from standard must be precisely identified, located, and described.* The technical man stated the deviation as "carbon simultaneously deposited on all 480 filaments of machine No. 1, starting about 3:52 A.M. and lasting for ten minutes." To insure precision, a problem analyzer specifies what the problem is by describing it very accurately in terms of four dimensions: identity, location, time, and extent. He also describes what the problem does *not* include and thus draws a boundary around it to distinguish its exact area.

4. *There is always something distinguishing that which has been affected by the cause from that which has not.* Carbon showed on the filament of machine No. 1 while the filament from the other machines was not affected. One thing distinctive about machine No. 1, as opposed to the others, was the location of its individual air intake. To uncover such distinctions a manager analyzes the specification of the problem, comparing the characteristics of what has and what has not been affected. He looks for what sets apart that which was affected from that which was not.

5. *The cause of a problem is always a change that has taken place through some distinctive feature, mechanism, or condition to produce a new, unwanted effect.* Only those changes connected with distinctive areas of the deviation are relevant and to be considered; thus coal soot from the switch engine was a relevant change in the filament

case because it had an unwanted effect through certain distinctive features. Blowing the stacks of the boiler plant was not a relevant change because its effect was not such as to be limited to areas of distinction. To find *relevant* changes, the manager looks closely at each distinction he identifies in his specification of the problem.

6. *The possible causes of a deviation are deduced from the relevant changes found in analyzing the problem.* The plant manager deduced that "something like a locomotive," i.e., the switch engine, could have been a possible source of the offending carbon which was the cause of the blackened filament. Such deductions enable the problem analyzing manager to establish a testable statement or proposition as to the possible cause of a problem, e.g., "Coal soot from a switch engine stopping under the air intake of machine No. 1 between 3:52 A.M. and 4:03 A.M. could have caused the blackened filament."

7. *The most likely cause of a deviation is one that exactly explains all the facts in the specification of the problem.* Thus the managers checked the first possible cause of blackened filament (soot from the boiler plant) and found this did not fit with the fact about the time of the deviation (3:52 to 4:03 A.M.), or with the fact that only one of the six machines sucked in the soot. But when they checked the second possible cause (soot from a switching engine) they found that this would exactly account for every detail of the problem as they had specified it.

In a similar way, the basic concepts of decision making follow a rational progression. There are, of course, marked differences. Problem analysis produces an explanation that

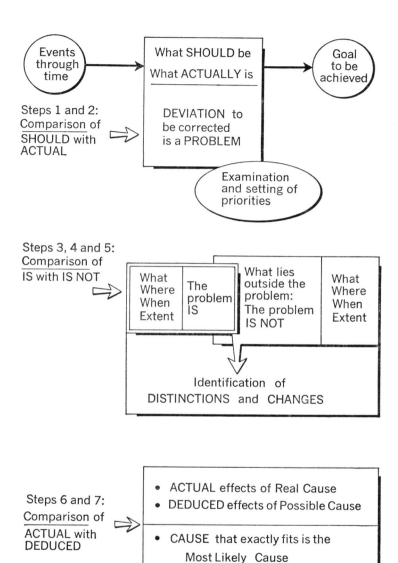

FIGURE 7 The seven steps of problem analysis involve a series of comparisons made with various parts of the information available. These comparisons are made in order to arrive at a cause-and-effect conclusion that is the most tenable one possible.

can be verified because the event (the cause) has already taken place; but decision making gives answers that cannot be verified because the actions will take place in the future, which is always uncertain. Nevertheless, the manager handling problems has to choose action of one kind or another, and if he has systematically identified and verified the cause of a problem, he will be in a position to make sure that the action he decides on will actually take care of that specific problem, temporarily or permanently. Making the best decision will involve a sequence of procedures based on the following seven concepts:

1. *The objectives of a decision must be established first.* What is the manager trying to accomplish? What is the job to be done? In the filament case, the objectives could have been stated thus: "To prevent carbon from getting into the machines, and to do this cheaply and with little upkeep or maintenance."

2. *The objectives are classified as to importance.* Preventing carbon from getting into the machines would be a "must," a requirement that cannot be compromised. Doing this at low cost and with little maintenance would be two "wants." "Wants" are not requirements but are open to bargaining where the manager would like to have the best performance possible out of the decision. The "wants" are then ranked and weighted, e.g., if low cost were more important to management, this "want" would carry a heavier weighting in the final decision than the ease of maintenance.

3. *Alternative actions are developed.* These are different ways of getting the specific job done, and many alterna-

tives are always available, some cheaper or better than others. In the filament case alternative actions that could keep carbon out of the machines would be: (a) installing air-filtration equipment; (b) moving the air intakes to the roof; (c) instructing the train crew never to park behind the filament extrusion building; (d) asking the railroad to use a diesel switcher in the yards.

4. *The alternatives are evaluated against the established objectives.* Each alternative is assessed as to whether it satisfies each of the "musts" (e.g., keeping carbon out) and as to how well, relative to each of the other alternatives, it achieves each of the "wants" (e.g., low cost, easy maintenance).

5. *The choice of the alternative best able to achieve all the objectives represents the tentative decision.* The best alternative meets all the "must" requirements and gives the most of what is wanted with the fewest disadvantages; it is the action that, on balance, does the total job best. The choice may call for a combination of alternatives; for example, in the filament case the best solution would probably be to ask for a diesel switcher and also to issue instructions to the train crew.

6. *The tentative decision is explored for future possible adverse consequences.* An adverse consequence is a future problem resulting from an action taken. Such threats are assessed as to seriousness and probability. Consequences in the filament case could be: (a) the railroad might not always be able to supply diesel switch engines; (b) a train crew might forget and park under the air intake again; (c) direct instructions to the train crew might be resented

and disobeyed. If the threats from a contemplated action are too great, another decision may be necessary.

7. *The effects of the final decision are controlled by taking other actions to prevent possible adverse consequences from becoming problems, and by making sure the actions decided on are carried out.* Thus the adverse consequences noted above might be minimized or avoided by: (a) giving standing orders to the yardmaster to caution the crew of any steam engine coming into the yards; (b) alerting all concerned to the danger of soot coming into the air intakes; (c) sending instructions to the train crews through normal railroad company channels.

This summary of the basic concepts of problem analysis and decision making is intended only to show the form and application of each concept. A great deal more will have to be said about the concepts before the reader has a working understanding he can use as a management tool. However, the foregoing summary should make clear the essential differences between the concepts of problem analysis and the concepts of decision making. Thus, problem analysis involves sharp observation, analysis, and specific comparisons—all aimed at *finding cause;* whereas decision making involves stating clear objectives, and carefully evaluating alternatives—all aimed at *taking action.*

The definitions of problem and decision in this text are made very explicit. A "problem" is always a deviation from some standard or norm of desired performance. A "decision" is always a choice between various ways of getting a particular thing done or end accomplished. It should also be made clear that a problem exists *only* when

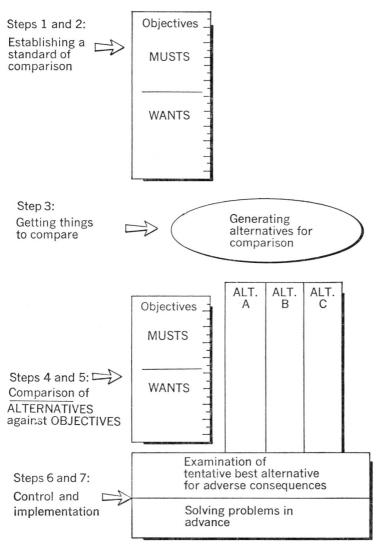

FIGURE 8 The first three steps of decision making are a series of actions preparing the information for the making of one complete comparison. This will determine the best action to take on a problem. The last two steps compare the expected results of this action against its possible adverse effects.

one or more persons think that a deviation from a desired performance should be corrected and are concerned enough to look for its cause, or think that the performance should be changed in order to meet a different standard. Obviously, if there is some departure from desired performance and this is of no concern to anybody, then no problem exists.

These definitions clearly separate the ideas of this book from the "creative problem-solving" approach currently in vogue. By these definitions, "creative problem solving" is not problem solving at all, but is more properly a method for generating alternative actions. Variously called "creativity" and "brainstorming" by its supporters, and "cerebral popcorn" by its detractors, it aims to achieve a great many novel "solutions" to a problem in the hope that one will work. And, in fact, this technique does sometimes produce a novel way out of a problem situation. But it does not lead to an understanding of precisely what is wrong, how things got that way, and what is the most economical way of correcting the trouble.

"Creative problem solving" deals entirely with generating alternatives. It begs the question of how one can possibly select the best, most rational action for correcting a problem when the problem and its cause are unknown or obscure. It makes the untenable assumption that the characteristics of the problem and its cause are unimportant. It leaps from "We have to do something" to "Let's go that way," paying little heed to the what and the why of the situation that impels the action in the first place. While "creative problem solving" may at times be useful as a means of developing alternatives, it should not be confused with the process of rational problem analysis and decision making.

Making these concepts and procedures work on the job requires diligent, persistent, and disciplined effort. It also inevitably involves intelligent, systematic thinking. There is no foolproof mechanical procedure for analyzing problems and making decisions that will relieve the manager from thinking. But once the concepts set forth here are fully understood and the procedures applied, they can provide real payoff for the manager. They can make him more efficient and accurate in finding the causes of problems, and thus improve his batting average in finding efficient, corrective actions. They can help him to use his own special experience more productively, and to handle new situations where he has little or no experience. They allow him to test the analysis of a problem and prove himself right *before* he has taken any action on it; and they can provide him with a visible record for checking his analyses *after* he has taken action—thereby permitting him to see where he succeeded, and how he did so, or where he slipped, and why.

All these benefits are implied in the phrase "using information efficiently." Specifically, it means that once a manager has identified a problem, his analysis of it can proceed in orderly fashion through distinct procedures. Each of these includes definite actions the manager takes in applying the concepts of problem analysis, i.e., the asking of specific questions and the finding of specific answers. It is these actions, along with the corresponding concepts, that will be presented in detail in the following five chapters.

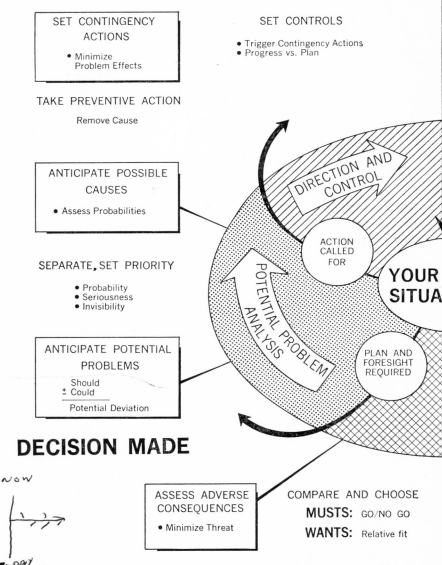

FIGURE 9 The action sequence for problem analysis and decision making. The sequence runs clockwise systematically around this "wheel," from problem analysis through decision making and potential problem analysis to direction and control. But a manager may enter this sequence at any

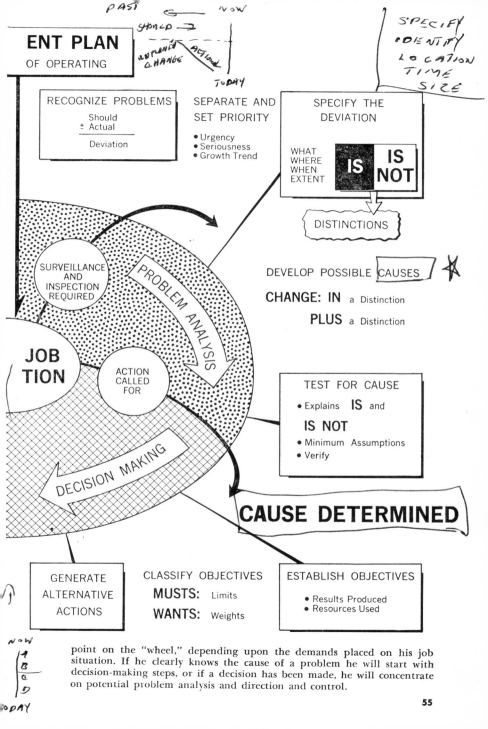

point on the "wheel," depending upon the demands placed on his job situation. If he clearly knows the cause of a problem he will start with decision-making steps, or if a decision has been made, he will concentrate on potential problem analysis and direction and control.

1. INFORMATION
2. SITUATIONS
3. SET PRIORITY
4. SPECIFY

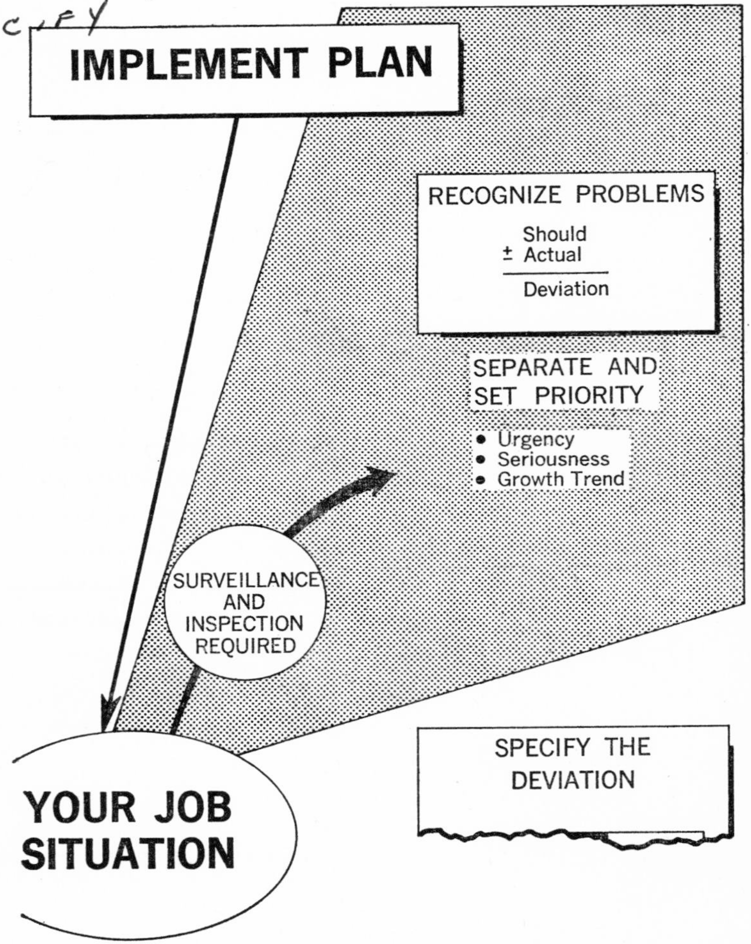

IMPLEMENT PLAN

RECOGNIZE PROBLEMS

Should
± Actual

Deviation

SEPARATE AND SET PRIORITY

- Urgency
- Seriousness
- Growth Trend

SURVEILLANCE AND INSPECTION REQUIRED

SPECIFY THE DEVIATION

YOUR JOB SITUATION

FIGURE 10 A manager starts the problem analysis portion of the action sequence by comparing what *actually* is happening against what *should* be happening. This enables him to locate deviations, the trouble spots to be studied. Any deviation he considers important enough to require correction is a problem to be solved.

CHAPTER **4**

Where to Start

Picking the right problems to work on may seem like a simple operation, which is probably why so many managers skip lightly over a series of problems and tackle those that at first glance appear to be the worst. However, the task is not that simple. It involves several actions and the handling of much information. To pick the right problem, a manager has to know what standards of performance he is following and what is actually going on in his department; he has to recognize when a problem exists and identify clearly the problems he wants to correct; and then he has to choose the most important problems to work on first. Doing each of these things well can increase his competence in problem analysis.

Consider, first, the recognition of a problem. Our definition of a problem says that it is a deviation from some standard of performance. A deviation from standard implies that some standard has been set, that someone has determined what the behavior or level of performance *should be.* For the manager, the standard set might be one of several—a company ideal or tradition, a rule, limit, or quota, a norm of ordinary behavior or common practice, a certain level of quality. The standard may be very specific, such as so many units to be produced per hour, or it may be as intangible as "conduct becoming a gentleman."

The standard, or "should," in management is usually directly related to a planned activity developed by, or known to, the manager. Therefore, he has to be clearly informed about the level and kind of performances expected, as set forth in the company's standards, practices, ideals, and norms. Unless he is clear about these things, he cannot be clear about problems.

In problem analysis, the manager needs to be clear about the relationship of the "should" to the objectives. The "should" is the expected standard of performance that must be realized if organizational objectives are to be attained. It is a measure against which actual performance can be gauged. It is not simply a standard based on past experience, nor is it "usual" or "normal" performance, which is merely the statistical projection of what has happened in the past. The "should" represents past experience plus something the manager wants to add to this to produce an improved performance. A good manager has to do better than barely beat last year's performance if he wants to stay in management. His performance standards will be derived from the objectives he and his company have established, in the sense that if these objectives are going to be accomplished at some future date, some definite performance standards must be met at this specific time. In effect, the manager setting performance standards tells himself, "On this day, if I am going to get to my objective, this ought to be happening."

Against this "should" he compares the "actual," the performance that is really occurring at this point in time. If there is a deviation between the two, the variation will appear when he makes this comparison. He must know what the efficiencies really are, what the attitudes are, the volumes, the complaints, etc. What is actually going on will often vary from what should be going on. Sometimes things go better than expected, and there is a positive deviation, i.e., the actual performance is above the standard set by the "should." In that case, the manager will want to find out why, so that such extra performance may be duplicated in the future. But generally the deviations are negative, below the standard set by the "should." Though the same analytical process applies to either case, it is the undesirable deviations that we are principally concerned with here. There is normally some allowable variation between the "should" and the actual performance, since managers know they cannot expect stable, nonfluctuating performance in any activity. Any deviation beyond this band of limits becomes a problem when the manager gets concerned enough about it to find out why it exists and to take action to correct it.

Thus two conditions must exist before a deviation is classified as a problem. First, the manager has to *recognize* that there is an undesirable deviation of "actual" from "should." If his band of limits is too broad, based on his past experience, and he sees no problem, then he has no problem. (His boss, of course, will undoubtedly have problems because this subordinate's standards are too lax to pinpoint poor performance.) The second condition is that the manager has to *want* to find the cause of something that is wrong and correct it. If the deviation from a standard of performance is large, and even troublesome, and the manager is still not concerned about this, no problem exists for him.

These two conditions are often related. For example, if a manager knows his boss is demanding high volume on a product even though this added pressure for output means a high reject rate, the manager may overlook the wastage involved, and so have no problem. The "should" in this case would be the performance expected by the boss. If the wastage violates the company's official standards, the deviation would be a problem only for those in the company who *wanted* to enforce these standards. In another case, the manager might set his own standard of expected performance higher than the company's standard, because of great pride in his work. He would then see and might want to correct a great many more problems than his boss did.

In any case, the manager has to decide which "should" he is going to go by, i.e., the company's, his boss's, or his own. Whatever standards the manager accepts (usually a combination of his own and his boss's), he uses these in turn to set the performance standards for those under him. He must be continually ready to review these standards to see that they are adequate. As one manager put it, "My hardest task is determining what the 'should' should be."

Problem analysis thus begins with the manager's own store of relevant information about standards that have been set and the actual performance he observes. The

manager recognizes deviations when he recognizes unwanted variation between what is happening and what
should be happening. His next step in problem analysis is
to identify those things that have gone wrong in his operation; then he selects those he thinks something should be
done about. He cannot hope to handle simultaneously all
or even several of the problems before him. Therefore he
has to set up some system of priorities to help him decide
which deviation he is going to tackle first.

He begins this by surveying the situation around him,
finding out what is actually happening in his operation.
With a good knowledge of the expected performance
standards in each area he can identify deviations from such
performance. But he will only consider those deviations
where he believes something is wrong, and which he wants
to correct. He will not waste time considering deviations
which are permissible within the band of limits he has
established for himself, or the company has established for
him.

His next step is to review quickly all the problems he
has located in terms of what he knows about them, i.e.,
what facts or information he has on hand about them. In
some cases, he will have a great deal of information; in
others, very little. Some deviations, such as a machine
breakdown, will stand out sharply and be unmistakable.
Others, such as one evidenced only by a small discrepancy
in a report, may not be easy to spot, though such a discrepancy might be evidence of a nearly invisible but extremely important deviation. For example, the production
vice president of a large rubber company, who had made it
his business to be aware of field complaints, learned one

morning that twelve identical failures of tire stems had been reported. These had not seemed serious to some twenty-five other managers who had read the reports, for ordinarily such a company will hear about hundreds of complaints every week. This vice president, however, saw at once that these twelve failures were unusual in character, and this alerted him to the possible consequences of customer claims, accidents, and insurance suits. So he dropped everything and saw to it that this problem was investigated. The failures were systematically traced to a change in the metal alloy that an outside supplier had recently made, and, by the end of the day, he had taken corrective actions, embargoing all stems from this supplier, and replacing them from stock. Had this problem gone undetected, it could undoubtedly have cost the company millions in damages.

In surveying problems a manager should beware of the tendency to lump a lot of them together under one title. This "clustering" of deviations is quite common and produces such inclusive descriptions as "communications problem," "the morale problem," and "productivity has fallen off." The "clustering" habit is a symptom of our tendency to associate similar things and assume that they are caused by the same things. For example, a "morale problem" might include these related problems: (1) grievances are increasing; (2) some men have recently quit; (3) new recreation facilities have been abused by employees. The assumption may be that all these have the same cause, and that together they constitute a "morale problem." Such an assumption only confuses and obscures the separate problems and makes the finding of their separate causes very difficult.

A tangle of different problems is often given a "handle" by which it is locally recognized. For instance, at one auto company the loss of the convertible car market (sales had fallen from 78 per cent to 12 per cent of the market) was referred to as "the convertible problem." Actually, this was a tangle of many different deviations. Unless the tangle of problems is broken apart into separate deviations, it may continue to baffle analysis for years. Such was the case at one big tire company where a problem of long standing was known as "the sidewall separation problem." Finally, the trouble was broken down into three deviations: (1) separation; on the flat part of the tire of tread from casing; (2) separation where the rubber had parted from the casing high on the side of the casing; (3) separation where the rubber had never stuck to the side of the casing

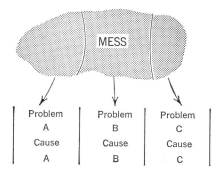

FIGURE 11   A number of problems tangled together is a mess. A manager cannot solve such a mess until it is broken apart into separate problems. Since each problem has its own cause, each should be analyzed independently.

in the first place. Once the three deviations had been described separately, the solution to one of them came immediately and very clearly. The second problem was solved a week later and progress was made on the third, which had up to this time been considered beyond solution.

Unless a cluster of problems like this is broken apart, a manager is likely to believe he can find a way to correct a whole tangle of problems at once. This is just not so. He might take a drastic action that would eliminate a lot of connected problems; for example, he might drop a poor product altogether. But he cannot escape the fact that each deviation has a cause, and he must find that cause in order to correct each problem. A cluster of deviations will appear to have several causes and require several different solutions. Therefore, instead of asking, "What's the problem?" where the answer could be simply a broad cluster of deviations, the manager should ask, "What's the deviation?" and thus sharpen the necessity for finding specific information.

In some cases, problems will be interconnected through a chain of cause and effect. A manager may recognize a problem, analyze it, and find its cause. Then he may be forced to ask the question, "How did the cause come into being?" Thus the cause in turn becomes a new problem to be analyzed and explained, and *its* cause may in turn become yet another problem for study and solution.

For example, the sales volume of the twenty men in a sales division had fallen off sharply. The men were unhappy and grousing about the new Inside Sales Assistant, recently promoted from salesman. A manager analyzed the

falloff in volume and found the cause: the men were dissatisfied and were spending more time grumbling than selling. Now the grumbling itself became a problem to be
specified and explained. He found the men were complaining because they resented the Inside Sales Assistant. This
complaint he next analyzed as a problem and found the
cause: the men all felt the Inside Sales Assistant was "throwing his weight around" too much, telling everyone else
what to do. Taking this as the next problem, the manager
found that the Inside Assistant was required to exercise the
authority of a supervisor without having been given that
official status in the eyes of the other salesmen. When it
was fully explained to the men that the Inside Sales Assistant's job had been changed to include supervisory responsibility, and when his title had been changed to Assistant
Sales Manager, the trouble disappeared.

Here the initial cluster of problems had been found to
form a cause-and-effect chain which after analysis looked
like a series of stair-steps, as shown in Figure 12. However,
the stair-stepping of problem to cause, with each cause in
turn becoming a new problem to be solved, can be
dangerously misleading. It is very easy for a manager to
speculate that the various problems before him are interrelated, and to assume causal relationship between them
when they are in fact not related. Without knowledge of
real cause and effect, one could build a case for "poor
morale" as being the "basic cause" of the sales volume
falloff in the example given above. Stair-stepping, however, can only be determined *after* problem analysis has
been carried out, not before.

Once the manager has made sure he has identified the

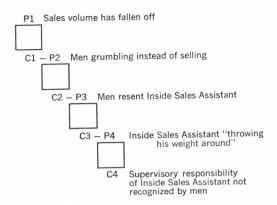

P1   Sales volume has fallen off

C1 — P2   Men grumbling instead of selling

C2 — P3   Men resent Inside Sales Assistant

C3 — P4   Inside Sales Assistant "throwing
           his weight around"

C4   Supervisory responsibility
     of Inside Sales Assistant not
     recognized by men

FIGURE 12   Diagram showing how one personnel problem (P-1) was stair-stepped from problem to cause to new problem in successive stages. In this process each cause becomes in turn a new problem to be analyzed, and this is indicated here by the box shown between each problem and its cause. Guessing at these problem-cause relationships cannot be done without grave risk of error.

problems he thinks should be corrected, he is ready to select those few deviations he wants to work on. These deviations will, of course, be those he considers the most important. To determine this, he will have to arrange them in some order of priority. To do this, he will ask three questions about each. The first question is: How urgent is the deviation? The second question is: How serious is it? The third question is: What is the trend of the deviation and its potential for growth? These questions will involve a series of subsidiary questions to probe out the answers. Thus, to answer "How urgent is the deviation?" a manager might ask himself: How critical is the time pressure behind this problem? How much time is there to get a decision? Is it a red-hot brush fire that cannot be ignored?

Can interim or stopgap action be taken to gain time for analysis? At what costs?

The question, "How serious is the deviation?" raises questions about impact. What are the effects going to be over a long period of time if this problem goes unchecked? What impact does the problem have on other people? On resources? On other departments? On safety? Will the problem generate future problems? What are the consequences of *not* giving this problem a higher priority?

The third question, "What is the trend of the deviation and its potential for growth?" raises questions about the future. Will this problem get progressively worse? Will it burn itself out and shortly disappear? What can be predicted for it? In answering such questions, the manager will be using his own judgment, of course. He will know that a slow-smoldering fire may cause much more damage over a period of time than a brush fire that flares up and then dies down. And a small fire in a vital location may do many times more harm as it spreads than a dramatically large fire on the periphery of an activity.

Also, a problem that in turn may cause other problems will be more serious than an isolated problem, other things being equal. The vice president of the rubber company cited earlier, for example, who spotted the failing tire stems, knew that by nipping this problem in the bud at once he was preventing a great many future problems that would be far more serious than the tire stem failures themselves. By going to work on this problem immediately, the vice president also showed he knew how to use his judgment as to how much time and energy he could afford to spend on any particular problem; he saw that this problem might not take much time to solve and its solution would eventually prove tremendously important in preventing a mass of costly insurance claims and law suits.

The manager's own efficiency is always a consideration. On which problem can he make the fastest progress and achieve the most important results with the limited time he has available? He can safely predict that it will take him less time to resolve a problem on which he has a lot of information than to solve one on which he has much less information. But he may, for instance, find that he has evidence that one problem holds the key to several others, and that solving it first may help him clear up the other problems more easily and quickly. Solving this one may also make the others seem less urgent. Moreover there is always the strong possibility that as he starts working on a few key problems he will uncover more information on other problems. On the other hand, if he starts on a long-haul problem and has to dig in for a lot of information, he may spend much valuable time before he can come to any conclusions at all, and by then he might have solved several more immediate problems.

Whatever priorities he sets, the manager should never consider them permanent and unchangeable. They are merely part of his starting plan for solving problems. As he digs deeper into his priority problems, he may well discover new information about other problems that makes them seem more important than the first group. Or he may reach a temporary dead end in working on his priority problems. Therefore, he should be ready to set these problems aside and move against others as his priorities change.

Shifting his ground like this, or even just putting a
tough problem aside for a while, often gives a manager new
perspective from which he can view a priority problem.
Thus in one of the big aircraft plants a manager had long
and strenuously been trying to solve an adhesive problem
that threatened to ground a lot of important planes. He
had tried about everything he knew to make some insulat-
ing material stick to the aluminum fuselage and hold securely under a wide range of temperatures during flight.
But the more he cleaned and buffed and polished the
aluminum surface in preparation for the adhesive, according to accepted practice, the worse the adhesion problem
became. So he set it aside and turned to another problem,
hoping to come up with a fresh approach. This shift led
him into contact with a research manager in his company.
As they talked about the new problem they discussed the
chemical nuances of certain epoxy resin glues. The research man mentioned that traces of oxide made for a better bonding; sometimes the addition of only 3 or 4 parts per
million achieved entirely different results. The research
manager described a particular adhesive used on aluminum, and this turned out to be the same type of adhesive
the distraught assembly manager was struggling with.
Whereupon they stopped work on the manager's second
problem and went to the lab to work on his primary problem. There they found that if they applied this adhesive to
oxidized aluminum instead of to clean, buffed, or polished
aluminum, it held the insulation tight. Putting the priority problem aside and shifting to another had helped
solve the manager's priority problem.

A flexible approach to problem solving, however, does

not mean a vacillating approach. A manager should be ready to change his direction, but he should only shift to another problem whenever a good reason for such shifting is apparent. Otherwise, he is simply problem hopping, working a little on this problem, then jumping to another, then hopping on to a third. This kind of fluid, hit-or-miss approach can end only in inefficiency and confusion, as was illustrated in Chapter 1. It is just this kind of approach that a systematic attack on problems is designed to prevent.

There is, finally, one basic point the manager always has to clarify for himself before he sets any priority on a problem. He has to answer the question, "Whose priority?" Is he going to evaluate a problem's importance only according to his own perspective and judgment? Or should he choose the problem that he knows his boss considers most important? Neither choice, of course, may be right; the company's long-range objectives might call for working first on a problem that neither he nor his boss would give first place to, given their own objectives. The manager should rely on his own judgment as to what is best for his company, and set his priorities accordingly, being aware of the different weights that can be given the same problem within an organization—just as he should be aware of the different standards of performance that can be held when he weighs his "shoulds" against those of his superiors.

Deciding the importance of problems is itself a good test of managerial competence. The temptation may be for the manager to work on a problem in an area which he himself feels most comfortable or most informed about. Or he may choose the problem that is easiest to measure, and pass up those problems involving difficult or intangible situations, which actually may be much more critical so far as the achievement of his own purposes is concerned. It should not be forgotten that a manager is judged not by the number of problems he solves, but by the importance of his solutions to the company's welfare.

Once the manager has picked the problem he is going to work on first, he has only to ask himself one final question about each: Is the cause of this problem known or unknown? If he is positive that he has the facts that identify the cause of the problem, then he is going to be able to skip problem analysis and go straight to decision making in order to find what action should be taken to correct the problem. But he had better be absolutely positive about the cause, for the most inefficient thing he could do would be to proceed to make a decision about a problem on the basis of a wrong cause. If he has a reasonable doubt about the cause of any problem, he should find out what facts are available so that he can accurately specify the nature of the deviation. In this specification stage, which will be considered next, the manager will be taking a big step toward positively identifying the cause of the problem.

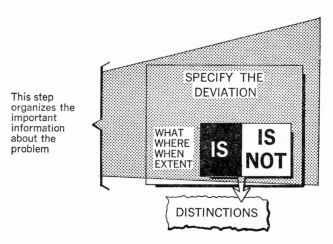

RECOGNIZE PROBLEMS

SEPARATE AND
SET PRIORITY

- Urgency
- Seriousness
- Growth Trend

This step
organizes the
important
information
about the
problem

SPECIFY THE
DEVIATION

WHAT
WHERE
WHEN
EXTENT

IS

IS
NOT

DISTINCTIONS

FIGURE 13   To specify a problem is to describe it so precisely that a boundary is drawn around it, demarcating sharply in each of four dimensions what the problem IS from what it IS NOT. This demarcation is necessary to uncover the distinctions that lead to the problem's cause.

CHAPTER **5**

How to Specify a Problem

It is true, as the saying goes, that a problem clearly stated is already half solved. It is also true that a problem cannot be efficiently solved unless it is *precisely* described. The logic of this cannot be refuted. How can you correct a problem if you don't know exactly what that problem is? No matter how urgent it may be, it will not be correctly solved without a very exact statement of what it is, and what its critical dimensions are. This pinning down the problem is what we mean by specifying a problem. It is not a blind hunt for "all the facts." It is a selected, careful search for certain kinds of facts that will draw a boundary line around the problem. This outline would include all that is relevant and important information about the problem and exclude all that is superficial and irrelevant. This dividing line will be drawn so tightly and precisely that it will expose the change that must be the cause of the problem. In addition, the specification of the problem will provide a standard against which any possible causes can be tested.

The kind of precise specification of a problem to be described in this chapter is, therefore, the most valuable single tool a manager can have for solving any kind of problem. It defines what is relevant, it exposes the clues to the cause, and provides a testing standard for every possible cause. The actual specification process is simple and systematic, even mechanical. However, the process demands firm discipline of the manager's thinking habits. No matter how strong his urge to look for the cause of a problem, he must stick to describing the problem precisely. Looking for cause comes later. For specification corresponds to the first step of the scientific method, which is clear and exact observation of the facts. Assumptions are to be rigorously excluded, or, if used in the absence of factual information, are to be labeled as assumptions and kept apart. Though this sounds easy, it demands a degree of thought and discipline that many managers do not habitually impose on themselves. Using a specification form, such as that illustrated in Figure 14, makes the job a little easier. Many managers have developed their own forms for helping them to deal with facts in their logical sequence and order.

To illustrate the need for an orderly, systematic approach to the facts about a problem, consider the Case of the Blackened Filament which was described in Chapter 2. Note that the technical manager eventually got enough facts to pin the problem down. He found that the black was carbon from an outside source, and was *on* the filament, not *in* the filament, and on all 480 strands from machine No. 1, and that the blackening occurred between 3:52 and 4:03 A.M. However, he then jumped to speculat-

PROBLEM ANALYSIS WORKSHEET

Deviation:

SPECIFICATION: IS	IS NOT	What is DISTINCTIVE of the IS?	Any CHANGE in this?
WHAT: Deviation, Object			
WHERE: On object, Observed			
WHEN: On object, Observed			
EXTENT: How much, How many			
Possible causes for test:			

FIGURE 14 A problem analysis worksheet used by managers in solving problems. It is really a framework of categories into which the manager sorts information as he digs into the situation before him.

ing about the possible cause of the blackened filament, for he asked, "How could carbon get inside machine No. 1 and not the others?" This question did not uncover the cause, but fortunately it stirred the foreman to produce some important distinctive information about the machines, i.e., that each machine had its own separately located air-intake system. This information then forced the technical manager to go back for more information by asking, "What is a local source of airborne carbon?" But this question led to another dead end when the stationary engineer reported that he had blown the stacks on his boiler long before the blackening appeared on the filament. Then the technical manager reshaped his question to ask about "a small local source of carbon that could affect one machine and not the others?" And it was this question that at last led to the cause when the plant manager guessed that the culprit might be the smoke from a switch engine, which turned out to be the case.

The technical manager's questioning would have been much sharper if he had developed a precise statement of the problem in the first place. The problem could have been specified by systematically getting answers to the following questions:

1. *What* is the deviation, and what is the thing or object on which the deviation is observed?

2. *Where* is the deviation on the thing or object, and where are objects with the deviation observed?

3. *When* does the deviation appear on the thing or object, and when are objects with the deviation observed?

4. *How big* are the deviations, and how many objects with deviations are observed?

All that can be said about any problem can be found in the answers to these questions. No matter what the problem, these answers will constitute the *only* relevant information needed for its complete description. But to make the description truly precise, what the problem IS must be sharply separated from what the problem IS NOT. That is to say, the specification should show both the IS and the IS NOT for each of the basic questions; i.e., what object is affected and what is not; where objects are found and where they do not appear, etc. The separation between such facts in effect draws a tight boundary around the deviation. More exactly, this dividing line separates those things and conditions that are affected by the cause from those things and conditions that are closely related but not affected by the cause. A specification of the Blackened Filament Case appears below.

	IS	IS NOT
WHAT		
Deviation	Carbon deposit	Any other blackening agent
Object	Plastic filament from machine No. 1	Filament from machines No. 2, 3, 4, 5, and 6
WHERE		
On object	Coated on surface	In filament material
Observed	On machine No. 1	Machines No. 2, 3, 4, 5, and 6
WHEN		
On object	After filament formed	Before filament formed
Observed	In bucket, starting at 3:52 A.M., going to 4:03 A.M.	Before 3:52 A.M. or after 4:03 A.M.
EXTENT		
How much	Heavy deposit	Slight or spotty deposit
How many	All 480 filaments	Some selected filaments

The reason for such precision in specification becomes clear as soon as the search is begun for clues to the change that caused the problem. Any cause is highly selective. This one had an effect on all the filaments in one machine and none in any of the five others, at one particular time and not at any other times. The change that produced this deviation acted on or through some factors that were distinctive of only that one machine and only that particular time. Whatever distinguished these particular things and conditions was connected with the cause. Thus the search for cause proceeds along two lines, in this sequence: (1) a search for those characteristics distinctive of the IS and not of the IS NOT; and (2) a search for changes that have occurred within, or have an effect upon, or are in conjunction with, a given area of distinction.

For example, in the filament case specified above, a sharp contrast stands out between the first IS ("carbon deposit") and the corresponding IS NOT ("any other blackening agent"). There is an unexplained cleavage between this IS and IS NOT. What is distinctive of "carbon deposit" here? Simply that there is no carbon found in the process or in the machine and therefore this carbon must come from outside the machine. Another sharp contrast or cleavage between IS and IS NOT appears with respect to location. This contrast shows up in the "What Object" category as "plastic filament from machine No. 1" but not "filament from machines No. 2, 3, 4, 5, and 6." This same contrast also appears in the "Where Observed" category as "on machine No. 1" but not on "machines No. 2, 3, 4, 5, and 6." Probing for the distinctions between machine No. 1 and the five other machines could have un-

covered the fact of a separate location within the building
with a separate air intake. However, this distinction, cou-
pled with the distinction of carbon from an outside source,
was not enough to identify the change. A third distinction
was needed, and this showed up in the "When Observed"
category in the contrast between the period of blackening
and the time before and after this period. What was distinctive of this period of blackening was the presence of a
coal-burning switch engine under the air intake of machine No. 1. This would have led to the critical change:
the presence of coal smoke in the air intake of machine
No. 1.

This example has been presented by quickly running
through the process to the location of the cause in order
that the importance of an accurate specification might be
underlined. The point and purpose of a precise specification is to highlight the distinctions and the changes to be
found within it. For that reason, it is very important that
the facts placed under the IS and IS NOT columns of the
specification be correct. The aim is always to specify those
facts that precisely describe, first, the deviation and the
objects affected, and then, those things closely related to
the deviation but not affected by it. The sharper this dividing line between what IS the problem and what IS NOT
the problem, the more likely one is to recognize those distinctions between the two sets of facts that will provide the
desired clues to cause. Thus in dealing with a problem
about products, for example, one would ask if the trouble
was in all of the product line or just with some of the
products, and, if the trouble was in all of the product line,
one would ask: "What is the most closely related product

line where there is no trouble but where one might expect it?" The tighter the line that is drawn about the problem itself, the sharper the distinctions will be.

Take, for example, the problem that was faced by a manufacturer of an automatic garage door that was electronically powered and motivated by a tiny radio transmitter in the car. The transmitter signal would activate the door, raising it if it were down and lowering it if it were up. The transmitter had an ultrashort range, so that one signal would not raise all the doors in the block. When the doors were first introduced in 1958 they were very successful, but as the fall approached and the weather turned cooler, the fog from the bay began to roll in and complaints also began to roll in. Such as: "Damned thing came right down in the middle of my new convertible—and I didn't touch the transmitter button!" And one woman phoned: "Come and take your door off; it came down and almost killed my husband last night."

The company, facing a major crisis in these complaints, proceeded to specify the problem. The specification showed that the complaints came in only on certain days but not on others, and particularly late in the afternoon and evening. Also, the complaints came from a single area on a part of land extending into the bay. This particular piece of information came out as they plotted the sources of the complaints on a map of the city. It soon became apparent that the complaints came from a strip of land cutting entirely across the residential section of the point. This area of complaints was wider at the ocean end and narrower at the bay end.

Once this specific outline of the problem area had been

drawn, the search for distinctions in the specification began. What was distinctive of the days when there were complaints as opposed to days when there were none? A quick check showed that days of complaints were days of heavy fog. What was distinctive of late afternoon and early evening? This was when the fogs rolled in, if it was going to be foggy. What was distinctive of the narrow cone-shaped strip of land from which the complaints came? This strip was directly in line with the end of the longest runway of a Naval air station located on an island out in the bay. Planes crossed that strip of land as they made their final approach.

Thus the distinctions found in the specification were "fog in the air," and "planes cross this area on final approach to the longest runway." Now, within, or with respect to, these areas of distinction, what changes took place? During the foggy periods the Naval air station flight controller guided the aircraft in to landings by radar, and he used a special radio frequency. He also used the longest runway exclusively for ground-controlled approaches. Aircraft coming in over the strip of land on foggy days also used the same special radio frequency. A check on this frequency proved it to be the same as the frequency used to operate the garage doors. Every time the Naval flight controller and the incoming pilot would speak to one another during an approach, their radio frequency would run the doors up and down. Once this was recognized by the door manufacturer, the door mechanisms were changed to a new frequency, and the trouble disappeared. After the fact, everyone recalled that all the doors had opened or shut about the same time, that there was always

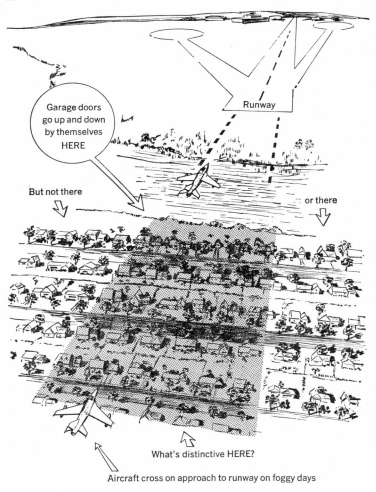

FIGURE 15   This diagram shows the distinction that led to the cause of a mysterious opening of garage doors in one locality. As the clues to cause, distinctions are a major tool of problem solving. If a cause has an effect one place but not another, there *must* be something distinctive of that one place to make this happen.

a plane overhead, and that it was always foggy at the time. But they had not recognized these things at the outset. Their experience didn't help them see the pertinent facts.

Similarly, a manager's technical know-how and experience cannot be expected to guarantee a precise specification of a problem in his area. Technical experience, in fact, can easily blind managers to the very facts that would lead to a solution. This was demonstrated in a plant of a large paper manufacturer where there is a pulping plant and a paper machine in line, with softwood logs being chipped and boiled with certain chemicals to the right consistency, and then fed as pulp into the papermaking machine. The plant was working well when suddenly it was discovered that small pieces of wood were coming through in the dried, finished sheets of paper. It was immediately assumed that something was wrong in the pulping process, that one of the huge stainless-steel screens had broken. Whereupon some $70,000 worth of new equipment was ordered to correct the problem.

However, one man was not blinded by his papermaking experience. He did not take the "obvious" explanation. Instead, he closely examined the troublesome wood pieces in the paper and found that these were not softwood chips but hardwood splinters; moreover, they had never been cooked or chemically treated. Then he spotted a hardwood pipeline used to transfer the pulp to the papermaking machine. He told his colleagues that the lining of this pipe must be breaking up on the inside and letting hardwood splinters get into the pulp mixture. His colleagues thought he was crazy because they had never heard of a hardwood pipe breaking up on the inside. But his explanation was finally checked out and found to be so, proving that the problem had nothing at all to do with the pulping equipment. This might have been determined at the outset if the problem had originally been precisely specified as "uncooked hardwood splinters in finished paper," instead of simply "pieces of wood in the paper."

Precise time can be critically important in a specification. For example, some time after one cocoa manufacturer introduced a new combination metal-and-cardboard container, loud complaints began coming in from housewives. They protested that when they opened the new cocoa cans they got a very strong disinfectant smell out of the can. However, the company found that other housewives using the same brand of cocoa in the same new cans had no complaints about odor at all. The trouble was only traced down after time was specified as one of the characteristics of the deviation. When the company followed up on the lot numbers of the cocoa cans that were bringing in the complaints, it turned out that the cocoa that smelled of chlorine disinfectant was distinctive in that it had been on the dealers' shelves for "three months or more." And cocoa packed in the same kind of containers and taken from the same lots, which had been on the shelves for less than three months did not smell of chlorine.

This distinction in shelf time spotted the change that caused the problem: the container manufacturer had begun using a new chlorine disinfectant to sterilize the wood pulp before forming the container, as required by law. This chlorine residue in the cardboard was liberated over a period of three months or more into the air space of the cocoa container, producing the disinfectant smell. It was an expensive change: the cocoa manufacturer collected $800,000 in damages against the container manufacturer.

The critical information that must go into a specification is not always easy to recognize. A good deal of questioning is often necessary to dig it out, particularly with respect to distinctions and changes. Such was the case with a major engineering and electronics company that developed secretary trouble after one of its reorganizations. The girls became dissatisfied, then unhappy, then furious. They complained that nothing worked, that the new typewriters they had been given were no good, that their desks were not level, that the air conditioning was noisy, and that management decisions were getting worse and worse. Attempts to specify the exact nature of the complaints led to much emotional catharsis but little hard data, as sometimes happens in situations like this. However, specification of "What Object"—in this case "who," i.e., the individual girls involved,—was somewhat easier. These girls turned out to be only about a fifth of the secretaries employed. Specifying "Where Observed" located all the dissidents in an older building—but not all of the girls in this older building were complaining.

Then it took a lot of probing to recognize what was distinctive of these complaining girls in the older building. The distinction was that all of them had been moved during the recent reorganization. Shortly thereafter the relevant changes were discovered: in each case, the girl had been moved from a new building to the older building, or from a larger to a smaller office within the older building. These changes were the cause of the problem: the girls were resenting the loss of status implied in the moves.

Nothing was wrong with the typewriters, desks, air conditioning, or management's decisions, with the possible exception of the lack of foresight shown when considering the moves. But as long as the problem was analyzed in terms of the complaints themselves, little progress was made toward finding the cause. As soon as the girls who were complaining were treated as the IS, and the noncomplainers as the IS NOT, it was possible to move ahead. Even then, the critical distinction was not recognized until after much probing. But then it became obvious: "Of course, why didn't I think of that before?"

These cases, and many more like them, repeatedly demonstrate how necessary it is for the manager to use both exact and inclusive observation in developing the specification. Since every problem differs somewhat from every other problem, the facts in a specification must represent the uniqueness of the deviation precisely, or the clues to the cause may be missed. As the specification illustrated on page 77 shows, the questions are all about what, where, when, and how big. The question "why?" is never asked, for this can only be answered when the cause is known. Asking "why?" is an invitation to speculate loosely about causes. If such speculation is allowed to enter into a specification, the tendency will be to develop facts that "prove" a cause which the manager suspects or has a hunch about. This does not mean that he need throw his hunches away, but he should set them aside until he has precisely specified the problem and analyzed it for the distinctions and changes that will lead him to possible causes. Then he may test his hunches as to changes that have occurred, along with the possible causes he has derived from his analysis.

As a practical matter, it does not take much time to set out the elements of a precise specification. He asks *what* is wrong and *what object* is affected; *where* on the object the deviation occurs and *where* objects with such deviation are observed; *when* the deviation appears on the object and *when* objects with the deviation are observed; and *how big* the deviation is and *how many* objects with deviations have been observed. A manager can then go through the facts about a deviation rather swiftly as he concentrates on separating what the deviation IS from what IS NOT the deviation but is closely related to it.

Once he has described and drawn an exact line around the deviation, he can proceed to analyze the specification for clues to the problem's cause. As already indicated, this process of analysis includes two stages: (1) a search for those characteristics distinctive of the IS but not of the IS NOT in the specification, and (2) a search for changes within such areas of distinction. These clue-seeking procedures will be spelled out in the following chapters.

RECOGNIZE PROBLEMS

SEPARATE AND
SET PRIORITY

- Urgency
- Seriousness
- Growth Trend

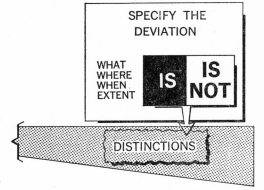

SPECIFY THE
DEVIATION

WHAT
WHERE
WHEN
EXTENT

IS

IS
NOT

This step throws
out of consideration
all factors which
could produce an
effect shared by
both the IS and
IS NOT sides
of the specification

DISTINCTIONS

DEVELOP POSSIBLE CAUSES

CHANGE: IN a Distinction

PLUS a Distinction

TEST FOR CAUSE

FIGURE 16   The cause of any problem is always a change that has had
limited effects, producing effects in some places but not in others. Such a
change is limited to areas of distinction or has occurred to features or factors that distinguish the IS of the problem. Therefore, to find which
change produced a given effect, it is most efficient to look only for those
changes that are limited to the distinctions found in the specification.

CHAPTER **6**

How to Analyze
for Distinctions and Changes

The search for the cause of a problem narrows down to the search for that change which could produce the precise effects observed through some area of distinction. This change may consist of several elements and conditions taken together as a complex change, or it may consist of a simple, single element. But in any case there is only one change, simple or complex, that can produce the exact effect observed. This change will be found through analyzing the facts used in specifying the problem. Analysis of these facts is thus the crux of problem solving.

Analysis of the specification to find distinctions is hard work. This is because we have all been taught to think generally in terms of similarities, putting things together that are in any way alike. When looking for distinctions we must do just the reverse, searching out what separates things, what makes them unlike. The problem analyzer must think in terms of dissimilarities. He has to ask,

"What distinguishes this fact or category from that fact or category? How is the IS distinctive compared to the IS NOT?" Then, in searching for changes, he has to ask, "What's new or different, what has changed about what is distinctive in this situation?" The ability to see distinctions and changes is one of the prime marks of intelligence, and it is critical in problem analysis. Even the most able managers can stumble at this point if they have not firmly grasped the concepts behind the finding of distinctions and the finding of relevant changes in a specification.

The concept of distinctions underlies the whole procedure of problem analysis. The manager has to find the one simple or complex change responsible for the problem, and the clues to this change lie in one place: in the characteristics that distinguish what the problem IS from what the problem IS NOT. It will be recalled that arranging information into the IS and the IS NOT produced contrasts between two sets of things or conditions, and that the purpose of these contrasts is to expose the distinctions. This exposure occurs when things and conditions related to a deviation on the IS side are seen to be in some way completely distinct from the things and conditions arranged in the IS NOT side of the specification. It is within just these unique characteristics of the deviation that the *change* is to be found that produced the effects specified.

A change is simply stated as something new or different. While many factors may contribute to a problem situation —set the stage for trouble, so to speak—there is one certain change that has disturbed the balance of forces and triggered the problem. Because this change has occurred in the presence of these contributing factors, the expected performance no longer is produced, and a deviation develops between the "should" and the "actual." The change involved may be simple or complex, superficial or essential, easy to spot or hidden behind other facts. But change produces deviation, and the critical change that is cause may best be recognized through the analysis of distinctions.

Now let us examine this analytical procedure in more detail in actual examples. In the last chapter we showed how the recognition of two distinctions led to the finding of a third and to the cause in the Case of the Blackened Filament. Under the IS of the specification the blackening agent was specified as "carbon deposit" and the IS NOT was "any other blackening agent." This contrast led to the distinction that carbon is foreign to the machine and the process, and therefore must come from the outside. Then in looking again at the IS and the IS NOT it was noted that one machine was affected while five other machines were not. What was distinctive that set one machine apart from the other five was its location; because its individual air intake had its own location, it was sucking in air that was different from the air being sucked into the other machines, since this air came from a different place.

Now note how the critical change that turned out to be the cause could be speculated once it was known that machine No. 1 had its own air intake. The question was, "How could soot get into one air intake and not the others?" And one manager speculated, "Something like a cloud of smoke from a locomotive." This led to the discovery of the third distinction, that which characterized the period of time during which the trouble occurred. This distinction was the fact that the switch engine had

been parked behind the building at that time, while the
crew came in for coffee. And from this point on, the determination of cause followed as a matter of course. The critical change was sooty smoke drifting into the air intake of
machine No. 1. The revealing question might more easily
have been asked, "What could have changed with respect
to the air intake to produce carbon inside the machine?"
And the answer could easily have been, "Why, soot or
carbon would have to drift into the air intake from somewhere, perhaps from a locomotive." In any event, the
discovery of the cause and the third distinction could
hardly have been avoided once the first two distinctions
had been identified.

In this case, recognition of one of the distinctions—the
fact that carbon came from outside the machine—led to the
discovery of the critical change that caused the problem.
But note that a second distinction, the separately located
air intake, acted as a condition necessary to produce the
specific effects of this change; that is, the location of machine No. 1's air intake *limited* the effects of the cause, the
blackening of filament on machine No. 1 only. In some
cases, however, a change found within a distinction *must*
be combined with another distinction in order to produce
the problem in the first place. This second distinction acts
as an *essential condition* for the production of the problem.
It has no change within it, and has no part whatsoever in
the triggering of the problem. But the change that does
trigger the problem cannot take effect if there is no second
distinctive factor involved. For example, there is the often-
quoted sequence of causes found in the saying: "For want
of a nail the shoe was lost, for want of a shoe the horse was

lost, for want of a horse the rider was lost, for want of a rider the battle was lost, for want of a battle the kingdom was lost. And all for want of a horseshoe nail." This sequence becomes significant only if we assume that there was something special about the rider of the horse, that he was bearing, let us say, a crucial message that would have saved the battle. Given this essential condition, an analysis of the problem would show two distinctions between the messenger's horse and all other horses on the field: this horse had a loose shoe and also carried the rider with the crucial message. The change that actually triggered the problem, and which was found in the first distinction, was the breaking of the nail in the loose shoe. But this change could not have produced the problem unless there had been that second distinctive factor involved, the rider with the crucial message. This second distinction *had* to be combined with the change found in the first distinction in order to produce the final results, which were the loss of both the battle and the kingdom.

Let us look at another example which illustrates other important points about distinctions. Here the manufacturer of a mobile radar unit had delivered the first sixty units of a large order, each unit costing $175,000. These performed according to expectations. On the next deliveries, however, the customer complained that the ball bearings in the base of the unit would not rotate smoothly on the bearing surface. The manufacturer at once made the common mistake: he decided to shut down production immediately and begin what turned out to be a long and expensive examination of the base assembly, lubricants, suppliers, etc. Finally, someone asked, "What is distinctive of the units from No. 61 on?" The answer: "They were produced during a period when we were overloaded and short of help. We borrowed some extra welders from another department to speed up work on the upper unit." Then this prime distinction was probed for a change, and someone asked, "Did this transfer of welders affect any of the work methods?" It was shortly discovered that these new men, not briefed on the details of the device, were clamping their ground lead at a different spot from that used by the experienced welders; they were putting the lead on the base of the trailer below the ball-bearing housing, and they were welding above it. The result was that electric current passed through the ball bearings and annealed them at points of contact; these burned points on the bearings and the bearing race were in fact the cause of the problem.

In this case it is notable that questions had finally revealed a prime distinction, but that no change seemed to be immediately apparent in the fact that extra welders had been put on the job. Nobody knew for sure that work practices had been changed when the borrowed welders came on the job. But someone then *speculated* that they might have, and this could be quickly verified. In other cases, sometimes no one even recognizes that any change has occurred, and the existence of the change may actually be unknown. Then a change must be speculated within the area of distinction, and perhaps combined with another distinction to establish the cause. The manager essentially says to himself, "I know about this area of distinction. If this speculated change were to occur within it, perhaps these results would be produced." The existence of the speculated change can be readily checked. When found to be factual, it becomes a known change to be treated as any other possible cause.

Now note how this ball-bearing problem could have been solved at the outset if a precise specification had been drawn up. The IS would have contained, "units No. 61 on," while the IS NOT would have contained, "units No. 1 through 60." The prime distinction between IS and IS NOT would have appeared much earlier: "period of overload, extra welders on the job." The speculated change in work methods could have been checked out immediately and verified: "ground lead attached below bearing race." The cost of not specifying this problem systematically was the cost of the production shutdown, plus the cost of units not produced and sold, plus the cost of useless research and investigation, plus the cost of poor customer relations growing out of the delay.

In general, the sharper the contrasts of the specification, the fewer the distinctions that will be found, and the quicker the changes will be recognized. If a contrast or cleavage between the IS and the IS NOT is sharp, and there is no distinction to be seen, then this is the sign that the problem analyzer must dig in hard and search, because a distinction *must be there*. In the case of the radar units cited above, there *had to be* some distinction setting "units No. 61 on" apart from "units No. 1 through 60." Without some distinction, there could be no effect limited to "units No. 61 on" and not observed on "units No. 1 through 60." Failure to find a distinction in a sharp contrast only says that the distinction is still to be found.

Failure to find a contrast in a specification, however,

indicates that the specification is probably not precise enough. In the case of the unhappy secretaries described in the last chapter, merely saying that some girls are dissatisfied, and some are not, will produce no useful distinction. It is only when the unhappy girls are identified by name and location that the real distinction can be found. Moreover, once the distinction is found, it must be precisely stated. The radar manufacturers could still be looking for the cause if they had labeled the distinction "busy as the devil" instead of "period of overload, extra welders on the job." Finally, when a distinction is found, it is also wise to ask, "Is this really so?" and to confirm the distinction rather than simply assume it exists. The distinction used must be a *known* distinction.

Problems are often made more difficult by the element of time. Time distinctions are therefore often critical in the solution of a problem. Thus the effects produced by a change may not be noticed immediately, and this time lag between change and observed effect may cover up the clues needed to relate cause and problem. Or it may be that time is required for the change to produce an effect, as was apparent in the case of the cocoa manufacturer described in the last chapter. There, a distinction in the form of the time that the cocoa had stood on the shelf made possible the discovery of the change that had been made in the disinfecting of the container some months before.

In other cases, a distinction may concern time, but not a time lag. For example, a pet-food manufacturer suddenly began receiving reports from all over the country that its canned dog food was exploding and the meat inside was rotten. There was no trouble with the cat food produced

on the same line. Ordinarily, the company had no trouble
with spoilage since all the pet food was cooked and canned
while it was very hot. So the managers of the company at
once started looking for causes and found that the production department had shortly before changed over to another method of sealing the cans on both products. Because this change immediately preceded the trouble, it was
assumed to be the culprit, and the can supplier received
some heavy criticism. But when the can supplier tested the
new sealing process in its laboratory, the cans worked per-
fectly. The deviation could not be produced experimen-
tally. Besides, there was no failure with the seal on the cat-
food cans. So this assumed cause of the bad dog food was
thrown out. Incidentally, this is a good example of the
potential risk in spotting a change and concluding that it
must be the cause of the problem, without first specifying
the problem and getting out the distinctions. Without
complete knowledge of the problem you sometimes cannot
recognize the answer when you have it.

Lacking a systematic approach to the problem of the
exploding dog food, this company spent considerable time
investigating other areas before it finally discovered that
the man in charge of cooking the dog food had, on his own
authority, some time previously increased the cooking
time and temperature of the dog food. He had heard someone complaining of a high bacteria count in the raw materials, and he arbitrarily stepped up the time and temperature "just to be safe." Here was the relevant distinction
between the IS ("dog food turning rotten") and IS NOT
("cat food"): longer cooking time at higher temperatures, producing more pressure in the cans. Within this

distinction the change to the new sealing process was the cause, since the new seal could not stand much higher pressure. The new cans leaked, bacteria got inside as the cans cooled, and fermentation started. Note that this change could not have been caught in the previous laboratory tests of the new sealing process, because the laboratory used the normal temperatures and cooking times.

Often one of the smallest and seemingly most inconsequential details will be the one that identifies a distinction that points to the change that caused the problem. For instance, a man holding an important post in a large organization began to slip badly in the performance of his job. This man—we'll call him Joe—began to miss deadlines, failed to follow through on details, blew up before his superiors several times, and came in to the office later and later, sometimes not at all. After six months of this, with matters getting progressively worse, a group of his superiors met to decide whether Joe should be separated or not. They discussed the demands and pressures of his job, what they knew of his family life, the extent to which he drank. They were leaning heavily toward a psychoanalytical explanation of Joe's case when one of them casually mentioned that Joe was the only man that he had ever known who had a rich uncle. This set Joe apart from other men, at least so far as this superior was concerned. Then one of his colleagues immediately spotted a change: "Why, the old uncle died about six months ago. Joe was his sole heir. So Joe's independently wealthy now!" And that was all there was to the problem concerning Joe. Having inherited something over a million dollars, Joe didn't care whether he did a good job or not. Having discovered this,

his superiors spared him the rigors of the psychoanalytic couch, and simply handed him an early retirement.

Some of the toughest clues to spot are those that call for a technically trained eye, where the complexity of the problem to be analyzed is forbidding. In such a case, it is not always possible to examine the evidence of the trouble, which is often fragmentary and contradictory. But it is just in this kind of situation, where identifying a distinction appears to be nearly impossible, that digging until a distinction is found becomes all important. For without some knowledge of the areas of distinction, any speculation as to possible changes that may have occurred is well-nigh fruitless. There are simply too many possibilities. A distinction must be found to narrow the search for change down to within reasonable limits.

This was demonstrated when three ballistic missiles had exploded out of five launched in a series of tests. Because of the military priority attached to the missile, hundreds of technicians began looking for the cause. The number of possible causes was enormous, and no one tried to specify the problem. But one man noted a distinctive thing about these failures: just before the explosion certain subsystems of the missiles had suddenly and completely stopped functioning. Information telemetered back from the missile showed normal functioning as the missile rose from the pad, but then these subsystems would suddenly go completely dead. "They die," the man said, "as if there were a little man inside who turned off the switch. Or cut the wires. This is unusual." So he then made an educated guess and speculated that the change occurring was some break in the flow of electrical current from one subsystem to another. Now he began to dig for more information about the area of distinction he had noted. He got out drawings of the electrical system of the missile and identified all of the connections between subsystems. Then he focussed on the couplings that were longitudinal to the force of the missile at blast-off. Each electrical connection had some kind of locking clamp to keep it from coming uncoupled during flight. He examined the specifications for these clamps and spotted six that he thought were weak. Failure of any one of these six clamps would interrupt the flow of current and cause the missile to fall. So heavier clamps were placed on these six connectors in the hope that this would correct the trouble. The result was that no more failures of this type occurred with this missile. The actual cause, or any direct evidence of it, however, was never observed at first hand, since very little is left to work with after a missile has exploded. Both the speculated cause and the corrective action based on it seemed right in this case, but neither could have been directly verified except at preposterous expense.

Speculating about changes is advisable only after efforts to sharpen the specification and the distinctions have failed to produce known changes. And once a change has been speculated, it should be verified, if possible. The manager should ask, "Did this change in fact occur?" Depending on the answers, it either becomes a known change, or can be thrown out. Similarly, speculating about distinctions sometimes becomes necessary when a sharp contrast between IS and IS NOT carries with it no known explanation. As with speculated changes, a speculated distinction can be verified. The manager should ask, "Does this distinctive factor really exist?" and the answers will determine whether the distinction is known, or can be disregarded.

But speculating about *both* distinctions and changes at the same time adds up to nothing more than sheer guesswork, no matter how logical these may appear. In problem analysis the first and most usual step is to locate a known change in a known distinction from analysis of the IS and the IS NOT. If this does not produce a good, possible cause, then one may be found by combining this change with another distinction drawn from some other part of the specification as a condition necessary for the change to have effect. Only after this proves fruitless is it advisable to go into speculation about distinctions and causes. For the more known factors you have to work with, the more likely the finding of the cause.

Finding distinctions and changes, as we pointed out earlier, can be tricky business. One difficulty is that these two procedures require a keener order of discrimination. It is relatively easy to see deviations between expected performance and what is actually taking place, and the IS and IS NOT elements of a specification are readily separated. But it takes sharp observation and thinking to spot distinctions between similar, related things, and to uncover changes that may be subtly concealed within the facts of the specification. With a little practice, however, such discrimination can be soon developed.

Finding the cause of a problem is another procedure with its own requirements. For the changes uncovered by the analysis of the specification are only *possible* causes. Each one has to be tested rigidly to determine which is *the* most likely cause. But first it is necessary to find those causes that appear to be the most likely, and that very important step we will examine in the following chapter.

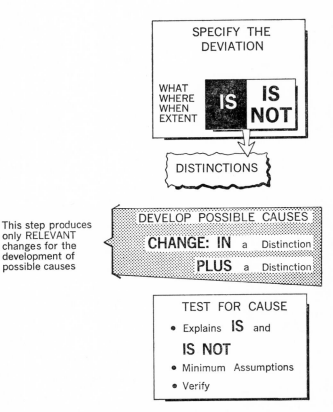

FIGURE 17 A possible cause is a provisional statement of cause and effect. The manager says in effect, "I believe this change produced this problem." He limits his statement of possible cause to those changes he knows or suspects have taken place within or in conjunction with a distinction he has found in the IS of the specification.

CHAPTER *7*

Finding the Cause

The search for the cause of any problem, as the examples in the last chapter indicated, is a search for the change, for that thing which is new, different, or unplanned that has upset the course of an expected sequence of events. The whole concept of cause rests on the evidence that there is an inertia of events, similar to the inertia set forth in Newton's first law of motion. That law stated that a body continues at rest or in uniform motion in a straight line except in so far as it may be deflected from that state by the operation of a force. In management, events proceed as planned unless some force, not provided against by the plan, acts upon events to produce an outcome not contemplated in the plan. The plan provides for what *should* occur, day by day. Problems are identified by comparison of *actual* performance against the "should." Finding the cause is determining what it is that produced the effect not described in the "should." It is searching out that which changed in spite of the plan. Not just any change; only that one specific constellation of events that could uniquely produce that observed outcome we call the problem.

This concept greatly clarifies the search for cause. It means, for one thing, that a manager who can precisely specify and analyze a problem can enormously simplify his search by restricting it to those changes that could produce that outcome, and by letting others go. He need only look for relevant change. He can avoid the pitfalls of the random, shotgun approach so commonly used. He need not rely solely on his past experience, which may mislead him; he does not assume he knows the cause of a problem simply because he knows about a cause that produced some similar problem. He can minimize the effect of his biases and prejudices about certain possible causes. He does not need to "brainstorm" the problem in the hope of stumbling onto the cause. He does not ask, "What are all the things that could conceivably cause this kind of a problem?" In trying to answer such a question he would spend most of his time considering possible causes that would prove to be completely irrelevant to the problem.

For the same reason, he need not try to list all the changes that may have taken place in his company at the time the problem occurs. If he did this, he would find a great many things had changed that had nothing at all to do with the problem as set forth in the specification, for everything is constantly changing. What he wants is the *one critical change* that caused the problem. To find this he must confine himself to those changes he can find that are related to the distinctions between the IS and the IS NOT of the specification. Whatever the change was, of all the changes that may have taken place, it had its effect within an area of distinction. It was, as we saw in one case cited in the previous chapter, a change that affected only those "units No. 61 on" through the use of extra welders, a fact which distinguished those units from others that were all right. With knowledge of the problem and its distinctions, the manager knows *where*—and where only—to look for cause. And he knows what to look for: *change*.

In short, the identification of the cause of any problem is not a matter of choice; it is a matter of systematically using the information and clues exposed through the specification. The relevant changes uncovered in the analysis of a precise specification will not be numerous; usually only a few such changes will be found that provide possible causes of a problem. These possible causes should be phrased in the form of *testable*, positive statements of cause and effect. For example, in the case of the smelly cocoa reported previously, one statement might be: "I think that something in the cardboard container has contaminated the air in the container."

The more specific the statement, the easier it will be, later on, to determine whether it is true. If more information is needed to make the statement more specific, then more information should be obtained. For, each statement must be treated as a hypothesis to be tested against the facts of the specification. In order to qualify as true, the statement has to fit the specification of the problem as observed, exactly, without exceptions or assumptions. We are searching for the change that did produce the effects, the facts set out in the specification. The test of a possible cause, therefore, is to hypothesize that it did produce those effects, and then see if there could be any exception to that relationship in fact. If you cannot "shoot it down," you must accept it as the most likely cause of the problem. The more time you spend on getting the specification precise, the less time you will spend in finding the cause of the problem.

There is no trick to generating statements of possible cause from a relevant change. The process requires thoughtful, careful use of information. It may also require some hard probing for information that others do not wish exposed. One difficulty that a manager may have in getting information about changes that have taken place may come as a result of efforts to deny changes that have been made. Some individuals may feel that the less they say about what they have done to change things the better it will be for them. Yet this is the very information the manager must have.

Sometimes the critical change that caused the problem may be so subtle or gradual that nobody is aware of it. An improvement in a product, for instance, is frequently overlooked as a "change." Or the evidence of the change may have been destroyed or disguised by the problem it produced; the changes that produce aircraft crashes are often of this kind. In such cases the manager can speculate a change as having taken place. He might say, "I think that condition X might have changed," and his judgment and past experience may give him a hunch that is persistent and strong. Hunches like this should not be ignored. If the manager asks himself, "What makes me think that condition X might have changed?" he may discover that his hunch took note of a distinction without his realizing it.

Then he can proceed to capitalize on his hunch by testing it against the facts of the specification.

Now let us see how these procedures of finding possible causes work out in actual practice. In "The Case of the Bad Butterfat" the problem developed swiftly, became critical, and was the kind that could throw a whole organization into panic. One morning the vice president of a major dairy products company, which we shall call the Reliable Separator Company, got an urgent call from the plant manager of Reliable's biggest Midwestern customer. The manager complained that the butterfat he had been receiving recently from Reliable's Midwest plant was so bad it had ruined the company's food product. In the last two days, merchants had been complaining and health authorities had impounded the product, so that substantial damages had already been incurred in customer goodwill. The manager said he had run a check on Reliable's bacteria counts on recent shipments and found them way above allowable limits. While some of the bags of butterfat were all right, many bags of it were putrid, and had apparently been running bad for the past week.

Faced with this threatening problem, the vice president's first reaction was to hop a plane and investigate Reliable's Midwest operations for himself. Fortunately he had the self-discipline to check this impulse; he realized he could learn a lot by phone, and even get some crucial facts that would escape him if he descended on the plant and many people got wind of the crisis. So he shut his office door and sat down to think the situation through. He reviewed what he knew about the customer and Reliable's butterfat operations. Reliable sold butterfat in bulk to this complaining customer at the rate of a truckload or more a day. The butterfat was taken out of the separators in semi-fluid state, put in sterilized 38-pound plastic bags, heat sealed, and then frozen to −20 degrees F. The frozen bags were shipped in precooled vans to this customer, a distance of about 100 miles, and during the trip the butterfat rose to −15 degrees, but this was still far below the temperature at which bacteria multiply. The customer used the butter-fat within a few hours, his quality control men taking a bacteria count on samples of each shipment when it was received. Reliable's own quality control men took a bac-teria count both at the time of packaging and when the bags were shipped.

The vice president started to write out his specification of the problem, and found he needed some more informa-tion. He phoned Reliable's Midwest plant manager and learned that no other customers had complained about bad butterfat, nor had there been any trouble in Reliable's own products made of this butterfat. The vice president hung up and completed his specification. After studying it he was tempted to jump to the conclusion that the cause of the bad butterfat lay in the customer's plant, not in Relia-ble's, because the customer had found no high bacteria counts in any but last week's shipments, and products made from this butterfat hadn't yet reached the market. However, he knew he couldn't prove this conclusion, so he proceeded to analyze his specification.

The problem was sharply limited, confined to high bac-teria counts in only some of the bags of butterfat sup-plied only to one customer, and only during the past week. He examined the specification for distinctions between the IS and the IS NOT and found only two: the customer was the largest user of Reliable's butterfat and the customer received butterfat in truckload lots. However, he could think of no relevant changes that might have occurred in connection with these two distinctions.

But he knew there must be a specific change that caused this problem, and because he had found distinctions in his specification, he knew where to look for changes. So once more he went after more information. First he phoned the customer and talked to the manager who had complained to him. Had the customer changed anything recently in its handling operations? The manager reported that nothing was changed; they were doing things now just as they had all along. He was very positive about this. So that apparently blew up the vice president's first conclusion that had put the blame on the customer. If they had made no changes, then the cause must lie elsewhere. Of course, the customer could be wrong, or could be unaware of a change that had actually been made. But for the time being the vice president had no choice but to accept the customer's word as true.

Then the vice president called Reliable's plant manager and asked if there was anything distinctive about this customer, or if the plant was doing anything differently for this particular customer. The plant manager said the butterfat was processed just the same as the rest, and handled just the way it had always been handled for that customer. How was it handled? For this large customer's convenience only, Reliable stacked the bags on pallets, and the bags tended to freeze together and were easier to handle. How many bags on a pallet? Forty-eight, i.e., six to a level and eight deep. Now the vice president knew he had another unique distinction for his specification: the pallet handling of butterfat bags for this customer. He pressed the plant manager for more distinctions of any kind he could think of, but none were forthcoming.

Now he asked Reliable's plant manager if any changes had been made recently. The plant manager said that about a week ago the takeoff temperatures of the butterfat at the time of separation had been stepped up from 75 to 95 degrees F. The reason given was that higher temperatures made the butterfat flow faster and allowed higher production for the busy season just beginning. A change had also been made in the sterilization procedure for cleaning the separators after each daily run, thereby lowering costs. Asked if there were any other changes he could think of, the manager thought some more and recalled several. A new quality control manager had been installed a month ago and he had changed the sampling procedure by having two samples taken at the same time as the butterfat went into the package. Also, new refrigeration equipment was now suspended from each bay and wall of the freezers to increase capacity; that was about three weeks ago.

With the additional data he had gathered, the vice president began to analyze his specification of the problem, which is set forth on the opposite page. He looked first for the sharpest contrast between IS and IS NOT. This was quite obvious; the high count was with X Company, not with any other customer or with Reliable's own products. What had he found distinctive of X Company? He jotted down three distinctions:

1. X Company is the heaviest user of our butterfat.
2. X Company receives butterfat in truckload lots.
3. X Company receives butterfat on pallets.

One other contrast that struck him in the specification was the contrast in "How Many"; some bags in a shipment were affected while other bags were not. The whole ship-

WHAT	IS	IS NOT
Deviation .	High bacteria counts, butterfat off flavor	Any other complaint
Object	Some of Customer X's butterfat	All of customer X's butterfat
		Any other customer's butterfat, or Reliable's butterfat
WHERE		
On object .	Some bags sampled, X shipments	
Observed ...	At X's quality control in X's products	Other bags sampled
		At Reliable's quality control
WHEN		
On object ..	At use, X plant	
Observed ..	During past week	At Reliable's quality control
	Products impounded, last two days	Before past week
EXTENT		
How much ..	Very high bacteria count, butterfat putrid	Within workable bacteria count
How many ..	Some bags in each shipment	All bags in each shipment

ment was not bad, just part of it. He knew of no distinction he could attach to the bags that spoiled as opposed to those that did not. Yet he knew there must be one. He speculated on this for a moment and then wrote down a fourth distinction:

4. Speculative: some bags of butterfat sent to X Company are more predisposed or vulnerable to spoilage than others.

This seemed reasonable and true, but, he had to admit, this speculation didn't tell him a great deal, at least not at this point in his investigation.

Now he examined the four distinctions for changes. There was none in the first distinction: X Company was still the heaviest user and the rate of use had not changed. Also, he saw no change in the second distinction: X Company still received butterfat in truckload lots hauled by the same trucking firm. Nor did he find any change in the third distinction: X Company still received butterfat on pallets, forty-eight bags to the pallet. So far, he was drawing a blank. What about the speculated distinction that some bags of butterfat are more predisposed or vulnerable to spoilage than others? A speculated change within this distinction would be that some bags become too warm, or are kept too warm, while others are properly cold. That would account for high bacteria counts in some bags but not in others. But he could not go beyond this.

Next, he considered the five changes that had been reported to him. None of them had been derived from the distinctions he had identified, but he thought they might lead to possible causes. He listed them:

1. The takeoff temperature at the separator was increased by 20 degrees F. a week ago.
2. A new sterilization procedure was instituted a week ago.
3. A new quality control manager was taken on a month ago.

4. A new quality control sampling procedure was instituted a month ago.

5. New refrigeration equipment was suspended in freezers to increase capacity about three weeks ago.

All that remained now was to frame testable hypotheses concerning each of these changes. How could the changes produce the effects described in the specification of the problem? He knew that to be testable, a hypothesis has to state, in a positive manner, that a certain change will bring about a certain result. It is a statement of relationship. And the test of a hypothesis is a logical one, using the facts available to determine if such a relationship is tenable. So he went over each of the changes that had been reported to him and wrote down tenable statements. He made these as clear as he could, for he was going to check each statement point by point against the facts of his specification. The hypotheses he came up with were based on three of the changes, as follows:

1. Taking the butterfat out of the separator at 95 degrees F. instead of 75 degrees F. allows the bacteria to multiply beyond limits before the bags are frozen.

2. The new sterilization procedure is not killing the bacteria in the separator, thus allowing the next batch of butterfat through the separator to become contaminated.

3. The new refrigeration equipment suspended in the freezers is not working properly, allowing the butterfat stored in the freezer to turn rancid before it is frozen.

He found that he could make no positive statements of cause and effect based on the other two changes, i.e., on the advent of the new quality control manager, and the installation of a new sampling procedure. These changes might well account for the rise in bacteria count not being caught by Reliable's laboratory, but they would not explain the high bacteria count itself. It did not seem at all likely that either the new quality control manager or the new sampling procedure were introducing contamination into the butterfat in huge amounts. Nevertheless the vice president decided he would not forget these two changes, but would hold them in abeyance.

He then turned to the speculated change in the speculated area of distinction. Speculating on both a change and a distinction at the same time is sheer guesswork, as was pointed out in the preceding chapter, but the vice president wanted to search for more information about this distinction and this change because they seemed to account for one of the striking facts in his specification, i.e., the fact that some bags of butterfat were spoiled and not others. So he thought about the speculated distinction that some bags were more predisposed or vulnerable to spoilage than others, and the speculated change that some bags might become too warm, or be kept too warm, while others were cold as they should be. He visualized the pallet with forty-eight bags stacked on it. Some bags would be on the outside exposed directly to the cold of the freezer, and some bags would be on the inside of the stack shielded from the cold. Depending on the location of the bag in the stack, the butterfat in the bag would be subject to different rates of cooling. The center of the stack would remain warm longer than the outside. He now saw that he had a distinction that was no longer speculative: some bags of butterfat *had* to be more predisposed or vulnerable to spoilage than others because some bags had to be on the inside, some on the outside, of the stack.

Now he also revised his notion of the speculated change to incorporate this information and to make use of one of the known changes in procedure reported to him. Given a hot center in the stack, he told himself, butterfat at 95 degrees F. would take considerably longer to cool on the inside of the stack than it would on the outside. So he wrote down his fourth hypothesis, which was an extension of the first:

> 4. Taking the butterfat out of the separator at 95 degrees F. instead of 75 degrees F., *and* stacking the bags on a pallet before cooling, allows bacteria in the butterfat *at the center of the stack* to multiply beyond limits; whereas butterfat at the outside of the stack is frozen before bacteria may have a chance to multiply to any serious extent.

Though the vice president felt most confident about the fourth hypothesis, he was still not jumping to any final conclusions. For he immediately began to wonder why neither his own quality control men nor the customer's had caught this trouble before yesterday. Maybe the No. 4 hypothesis wasn't so good after all? But he could not think of any others that were better than the ones he had put down. In any case, he was going to have to test each of these explanations rigorously, and he knew that during this process of testing he might very well run across some more information that would give him, finally, the complete answer as to the cause of his problem. As we shall see in the next chapter, this is what actually happened.

RECOGNIZE PROBLEMS

SEPARATE AND
SET PRIORITY

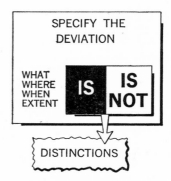

SPECIFY THE
DEVIATION

WHAT
WHERE
WHEN
EXTENT

IS

IS
NOT

DISTINCTIONS

DEVELOP POSSIBLE CAUSES

CHANGE: IN a Distinction

PLUS a Distinction

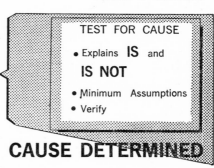

This step tests the
validity of the logic
behind "I think this
is the cause." Would
it really produce the
effects described?

TEST FOR CAUSE

• Explains IS and
IS NOT

• Minimum Assumptions
• Verify

CAUSE DETERMINED

FIGURE 18 A cause is considered to be the most likely one when it explains both the effects that were observed (the IS) and the absence of effects where none were observed (the IS NOT). The most likely cause does not depend upon a lot of special assumptions. It can also be independently verified in most cases.

CHAPTER **8**

Testing the Cause You Have Found

The major error that managers commit in problem solving is jumping to a conclusion about cause. They identify a problem, then say, "I think this is the cause of it." Then they compound the error in these ways:

- They collect arguments in support of their pet theory.
- They build a case for it.
- They become convinced that they have a complete explanation.
- They resist any other explanations of the problem.
- They have pride of authorship in their theory.
- They fight to protect it from detractors and critics.

To avoid this error of jumping to a conclusion about cause, managers need to develop a way of vigorously testing their explanation to determine whether or not it is the real cause. They need a way of being sure that they are not basing the decisions they will make upon a false notion of what produces the problem. Most of all, they need to turn their thinking around to test their reasoning, to try to find flaws or shoot holes in the explanation they have come up with, rather than bolster and protect it at all costs.

This about-face, this willingness to disprove a possible cause instead of supporting it with arguments, is the real key to finding the cause. Testing is actually the process of searching for any exception that can be found to any possible explanation of a problem. It is placing a possible cause in the change-effect equation to see if it will completely and exactly produce the known characteristics of the problem. Thus, it is the specification that positively tests the cause. Ideally, if a statement of possible cause exactly fits *all* the facts in the IS and the IS NOT of the specification, then this must be the statement of the cause that produced the problem in the first place. For there can be only one change, simple or complex, that is the cause of any problem, and this cause will have produced the exact effects as precisely specified, without exceptions and without assumptions. In most cases, because of incomplete knowledge of the relevant information, the best that the manager can do is to test to find the most likely cause.

It is the manager's job to make sure that every possible cause is tested accordingly. Because he usually has somewhat incomplete information, he has to examine closely each hypothesis, looking for loopholes, for inconsistencies, for exceptions, for partial explanations. Taking a well-rationalized explanation and methodically picking it apart can be a painful process when the explanation is one's own brainchild. Yet, a manager must be as critical and objective as possible if he wants to keep from fooling himself by settling for a false explanation. He has to beware of tacking "Yes, but under certain conditions..." qualifications onto his explanations in an effort to make them fit. Such qualifications are sneaky, tending to be made first in a disbelieving half-apologetic manner. The next time the qualification is stated it is given the status of fact. And the next time, it is gospel truth. A manager may be so relieved to get off the hook, to find a way around a troublesome exception, that he will take the flimsiest excuse to bolster a shaky hypothesis. Unfortunately, this does not solve problems; it makes more of them.

A possible cause that doesn't quite fit the specification may be true, but it may also be false. The best bet in such cases is to sharpen up the specification, improving the accuracy of details, such as replacing "black filament" with "carbon deposit." A sharpened specification will eliminate false possible causes by exposing their inconsistencies; it will also improve the consistency of a possible cause that is most likely to explain the cause of the problem. The specification is always the testing pattern; the more precise it is, the less uncertainty there will be in testing causes against it.

To qualify as the most likely cause, the statement of it must explain both sides of the specification, the IS and the IS NOT, logically, simply, and completely. Let us see how these criteria were applied to the four possible causes set down by the vice president who specified and analyzed the Butterfat Case described in the last chapter.

After ordering all further shipments to Customer X held up, the vice president began a systematic analysis of what he knew about the problem. The first statement of possible cause he had put down was: "Taking the butterfat out of the separator at 95 degrees F. instead of 75 degrees

F. allows the bacteria to multiply beyond limits before the bags are frozen." Would this possible cause produce the problem as he had specified it, both IS and IS NOT? He turned to his specification to test this cause against it, point by point.

The first entry in his specification was, "high bacteria counts, butterfat off flavor." If the 20 degree F. extra temperature at takeoff would produce high counts, this would account for the deviation as noted on both the IS and the IS NOT sides of the specification. So far, the explanation checked. Then he looked at the IS entry on "What Object": "Some of Customer X's butterfat." If the 20 degree F. extra temperature were the cause of high counts, these would appear in all the butterfat tested, not just Customer X's butterfat. So this cause would not produce the effect as noted on the IS side, nor would it account for the nonappearance of high counts in other customers' products and in Reliable's own products. Nor would this cause account for the "Where on Object" entries of the specification: "Some bags sampled, X shipments" but not "other bags sampled." If the temperature were uniformly 20 degrees F. higher, and this were causing the high counts, then these counts should be found in all bags shipped to Customer X, not just in some. Now he skipped to the "Extent" entries of the specification and found himself seriously doubting that a 20 degree F. increase in temperature would produce "very high bacteria count, butterfat putrid." This could be verified quite readily. But on the basis of the evidence in hand, he believed that the explanation of the increased takeoff temperature had been proven invalid by the exceptions noted, so he put it aside.

He now turned to his second hypothesis: "The new

sterilization procedure is not killing the bacteria in the separator, thus allowing the next batch of butterfat through the separator to become contaminated." Again he asked himself if this would produce both the IS and the IS NOT that he had specified on the problem. If the separators were contaminated as the day's run started, the first butterfat through the separator might have been contaminated, with resulting high bacteria counts. But the contamination in the separator would tend to clear up as it was purged by the flow of milk products through it. If Customer X was always served from the first part of the run, then this would fit with the facts. And this would also account for some bags being bad while others were all right. But Customer X would have to be the first served each day in order that this explanation might hold up. He was aware of this as a "Yes, but under special conditions . . ." assumption. However, it could be true and it could easily be verified.

He looked again at his specification of the problem. Under "Extent," the two IS entries were: "very high bacteria count, butterfat putrid," and "some bags in each shipment." Would an incompletely cleaned separator account for *putrid* butterfat, for a *very high bacteria count?* Highly unlikely, he thought. A very great deal of rotten butterfat would have to be left in the separator overnight to contaminate a number of bags in the next day's run. He could not accept a change in cleanout and sterilization procedures as an adequate explanation of the magnitude of this problem. It simply did not make sense. Besides, his own quality control people should have picked this up, at least on one of the days. So he set this hypothesis aside as well.

The vice president now reread his third hypothesis: "The new refrigeration equipment suspended in the freezer is not working properly, allowing the butterfat stored in the freezer to turn rancid before it is frozen." But once again he found himself with a hypothesis that was incapable of explaining why some of the bags in Company X's shipment had high bacteria counts while others did not, and why other customers' shipments and also Reliable's products were exempt. If the refrigeration equipment in the freezer were defective, then all of the butterfat in the freezer would have been affected. Besides, the new equipment was installed three weeks ago; if it were defective, he would have expected trouble to show up before this. However, he realized that the new equipment may have been adequate for butterfat at the lower takeoff temperature but not at the higher. If this were the case, raising the temperature by 20 degrees F. would be the cause, and poor refrigeration equipment a contributing condition.

This left him with two hypotheses, both of which were deficient in some way or another. He turned them to his last hypothesis: "Taking the butterfat out of the separator at 95 degrees F. instead of 75 degrees F., and stacking the bags on a pallet before cooling, allows bacteria in the butterfat at the center of the stack to multiply beyond limits; whereas butterfat at the outside of the stack is frozen before bacteria have a chance to multiply to any serious extent." Would this account for both the IS and the IS NOT of his specification? He went down the specification, point by point.

"High bacteria counts" might or might not be produced, he thought, depending upon how slowly the butterfat at the center of the stack cooled. This would be a critical factor to verify. If a hot center in the stack were the cause of the problem, then the inside butterfat would be more affected than that on the outside. This would account for "some of Company X's shipment" being bad while other parts of the shipment were all right. It would also account for the absence of any trouble with other customers' butterfat or with Reliable's own products, in which cases no palletizing or stacking was involved. He noted that this hypothesis was the only explanation that accommodated this persistent peculiarity in the problem. But if uneven cooling were a result of the stacking method, then why hadn't there been trouble before? And why hadn't Reliable's quality control people caught the fact of higher counts at the center of the stack? Perhaps the increase in takeoff temperature would account for the trouble showing up at this time. But if a hot center produced putrid butterfat now, then at a 20 degree F. lower takeoff temperature there should have been some trouble, and there was none. And the fact that his own quality control people had missed the problem was still unexplained. He had two possibilities before him: he either had an untrue hypothesis which could not be proven, or he needed more information.

He decided in favor of this last possibility. He picked up the phone and again called the manager of Reliable's Midwest plant. "How are our quality checks made?" he asked. After some probing for details, he got the answer: according to the procedure set up by the new man, samples were taken to give the bacteria count at the time of packaging and at the time of shipment. But both samples were taken at the same time, i.e., when the butterfat was put into bags. One count was then made immediately; the other sample was held in the *laboratory* refrigerator at —20 degrees F. and was counted when shipment of this particular lot of butterfat was made. This was done, the manager said, to avoid the trouble of breaking one bag out of the solidly frozen block on the pallet, and then thawing it out to take the sample for the bacteria count. Besides, the manager explained, the sample held in the lab refrigerator and the butterfat bags in the freeze room were both held at the same temperature, so the bacteria readings would be the same.

The vice president saw now that this procedure would account for Reliable's failure to catch the high bacteria counts at quality control inspection: the bacteria had not had a chance to multiply at the time the samples were taken. He promptly gave the plant manager a short lecture on the need to maintain proper quality control procedures. But there was still one question about the quality control business that remained unresolved: Why hadn't the bad butterfat appeared before last week? If this had been the usual sampling procedure, the vice president said to himself, then he could have expected trouble long before this. He pondered this, and then he had a hunch. He thought: "If our quality control people were lazy about getting their samples from the frozen stacked pallets, then their counterparts at this customer's plant might be just as lazy." He decided to check on this, and phoned the manager at the customer's plant, explaining what he had found out so far and describing Reliable's sampling procedures. How, he asked, did their quality control people handle the sampling?

The manager said he'd check, and within an hour called the vice president back. He reported that the sample taken on receipt of each shipment was always taken from an outside bag of butterfat, because it would be too hard to dig into the center of the stack of frozen palletized bags. The vice president's hunch about the laziness of both groups of quality control people was verified. But the manager at once tried to support the sampling practice by pointing out that the butterfat was presumably all the same in each shipment. If it was not, this was Reliable's fault. After the flavor of the product had gone bad, he said, his people had begun taking many more samples. However, these had been taken after the bags had been thawed out, so they couldn't tell what part of the frozen stack the samples had come from. All they knew was that some butterfat was good, and some was bad.

This information still left unexplained the fact that the customer's butterfat hadn't gone bad until last week. If there had been uneven cooling of the butterfat and poor quality control from the beginning, then, the vice president told himself, the customer could have expected bad flavor right along. That just hadn't been so. But why not? Suddenly, he realized that he had been in trouble all along but hadn't known it. The problem had been with him for some time but hadn't been recognized. Bacteria counts in the center of the stacked bags had been above the safe limits ever since they had started palletized shipments. The customer had missed recognizing this because of poor quality control sampling. The bad butterfat, diluted with good butterfat and other ingredients, had not shown up in Customer X's later quality control testing to an extent that would have raised questions as to its purity. Now he saw that the critical change was the increase in takeoff temperature last week that must have raised the bacteria count in the center bags to a point where the butterfat turned putrid and spoiled the taste of the customer's product. He could have verified this with more tests, but he didn't feel he needed to, right then. Everything in the hypothesis fitted the facts in his specification, and he was sure he had nailed down the cause of the problem.

He now ordered an experiment to verify his reasoning and his use of the facts on hand. He called the plant manager at Reliable and asked him to bury three temperature bulbs, attached to recording thermometers, in each of several palletized stacks of butterfat bags. One bulb was to be in the very center, one halfway out, and the third just at the periphery of each stack. The stacks were to be handled as usual and the data from the recording thermometers was to be phoned to him when the innermost thermometer registered —20 degrees F. Then the stacks were to be opened and a direct bacteria count made of the butterfat at the center, halfway out, and at the edge of each stack.

Some hours later the plant manager reported back, for it took a surprisingly long time for an entire stack to cool to —20 degrees F. The temperature record from the outside bulb showed a rapid fall as the butterfat froze, but the bulb placed halfway inside the stack showed much more leisurely cooling, while the bulb at the center registered only a very gradual fall in temperature. The plant manager also reported that within a few minutes after the stack had been placed in the freezer, the spaces between the bags of butterfat had become choked with frost and ice. The vice president, recognizing that frost and ice is excellent insulation, realized that the solidness of the block of bags had become a barrier to the dissipation of heat

Deviation: *Some of Customer X's butterfat is bad*

	IS	IS NOT	What is DISTINCTIVE of the IS?	Any CHANGE in this?
WHAT: Deviation	High bacteria count	Any other complaint	Function of heat	
Object	Some butterfat shipped to Customer X	All butterfat shipped to Customer X; any to other customers; Reliable's products	Selective of *part of* shipment	
WHERE: On object	Some bags, Customer X	Other bags, Customer X	Part of shipment affected	
Observed	At Customer X's plant	Other customers' plants; in Reliable's plants	X is heavy user / X gets truckload lots / (X gets pallet handling)	
WHEN: On object	At use, Customer X's plant	At quality check, receiving inspection		
Observed	Over the last week; product impounded last 2 days	Before last week; before last 2 days	Busy season beginning	(Takeoff temp. ↑20) / New sterilization
EXTENT: How much	Very high bacteria count; some butterfat is putrid	Marginal count	Function of heat	
How many	Unknown number, but many bags bad	Just a few, rare bags		
Possible causes for test:	Increased takeoff temperature makes butterfat too slow in cooling			
	Separator not fully cleaned at end of run, contaminates next day's butterfat			
	Hotter butterfat in palletized stacks makes center too slow to cool			

FIGURE 19 An ideal specification of the Butterfat Case, based on the information available. Note that in this specification the observations under the IS and the IS NOT are more precisely worded than the vice president's specification shown on page 111, and also some of the changes reported by Reliable's plant manager do not even appear here. The only changes that do show up come from the time period and its distinction, "busy season beginning." The cause turns out to be a change *in* this distinction *plus* another distinction, "X gets pallet handling."

trapped at the center. The direct bacteria counts showed the effects of this slow cooling very dramatically: the butterfat at the center showed an exceedingly high count—in fact, the plant manager reported that it was quite putrid.

The vice president's confidence in his analysis of the problem was justified. In his testing of the four possible causes, he had checked each carefully against his specification of the problem to see that the problem was explained fully, both the IS and the IS NOT, and with a minimum of "Yes, but under certain conditions . . ." assumptions. He had looked for exceptions, trying to find holes in each theory. He had kept going back for more relevant information to tighten up his specification. He had made some assumptions, but had refused to accept any hypothesis just because it partially fit the facts of the specification. Most important of all, he had refused to "build a case" for any explanation; he had remained objective, testing and probing and carefully using the information he had at hand in the form of the problem specification.

If the vice president had wanted to be absolutely sure he had found the cause, he could have further verified his findings by running tests on actual shipments. However, such verification is rarely essential, and in many cases it is highly impractical either for economic reasons or because of time pressures. In the Butterfat Case, the vice president wanted to eliminate the cause of the customer's complaints as fast as he could, and he did solve this problem very speedily. Once he had found the cause, he began making decisions and took these six separate actions: (1) the take-off temperature was reduced immediately to 75 degrees F.; (2) overtime was authorized to take up the slack in production caused by a slower flow of the butterfat; (3) the

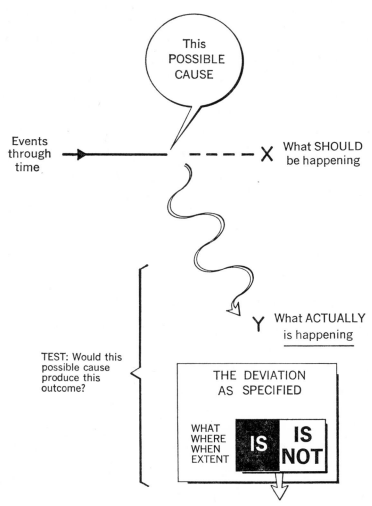

FIGURE 20 Testing a possible cause is the process of mentally putting it into the flow of events through time to see if it would produce *exactly* what has been specified as the deviation. The actual cause, of course, would agree in all respects with the IS and the IS NOT because it actually produced them. Without complete information about a possible cause, perfect agreement between the available information and the specification is not possible, and a cause can only be stated as "most likely."

palletizing procedure was changed, putting fewer bags in each pallet and leaving a 1-inch space between the bags; (4) he ordered a special test made to determine that the preceding changes would correct the deviation; (5) he phoned the manager at the customer's plant to explain his findings, and to describe the actions that were taken to eliminate the problem and prevent its recurrence in the future; (6) he made sure that proper quality control procedures were spelled out for each plant. *Result:* the customer did not sue for any damages, and remained a good customer.

The elapsed time between the first phone call received from the complaining customer and the completion of the corrective actions was exactly thirty-six hours. It is also notable that the vice president had no special know-how or detailed technical information about this problem. He relied instead on a thorough knowledge of the process of problem analysis. And he showed he had developed the essential willingness to shoot down his own theories as to possible causes of the problem.

His decisions about handling the problem were equally good. He made an interim decision to hold up further shipments to Customer X pending determination of the cause of the problem. He found what was causing the problem, then proceeded to correct it with specific actions. He included a control in his set of decisions to verify that his corrective actions were indeed effective. And he solved some future problems by anticipating Customer X's need for assurance that the problem would not happen again. These matters of decision making will be discussed in the last two chapters.

CHAPTER 9

Applications on the Job

How do these concepts and procedures of problem analysis work on the job? Managers who have studied them and practiced using them in a training group are often able to apply this knowledge as soon as they get back on the job. If a manager merely promises himself that he will use these concepts and procedures on the first big problem that comes along, he is likely to slip right back into the old familiar groove of thinking about problems, causes, and decisions in a very unsystematic way. This is unfortunate and unnecessary. For systematic problem analysis is not a rigid process; it does not have to be applied exactly as it has been described in this text. The manager who waits until he has a chance to apply the procedures exactly as he learned them is likely to overlook many opportunities for getting quick results on a problem. Some of the most effective applications have been anything but complete in the textbook sense. Sometimes only one or two of the concepts or procedures may be used in analyzing a problem.

The important point for the manager to keep in mind is

that he can apply some of these concepts and procedures whenever he runs across a situation that demands the rational use of information to achieve results. He could, for example, use some of these concepts and procedures in trying to improve the sales techniques of his staff. Or in getting facts that are missing in a strike threat. Or in showing subordinates how to approach an emergency situation. Or in trying to find out why the turnover is so high among certain employees. Or looking for legal evidence that will identify a particular person. Or in cutting down the endless hours wasted in staff meetings. These are some of the practical tasks that managers have tackled by applying systematic problem analysis.

In this chapter we will look at several cases of problem analysis and see just how managers have used the concepts and procedures. In these examples we will be primarily concerned with the analysis of problems, not with the five different kinds of action that can be taken in handling problems. Three of these actions will be described in detail in the chapter on decision analysis and two in the final chapter on potential problem analysis. Here it will be sufficient to present the following brief definitions:

Interim action: buys the manager time for finding the cause of a problem.

Adaptive action: lets the manager live with the tolerable effects of a problem or with an ineradicable cause.

Corrective action: gets rid of the known cause of a problem.

Preventive action: removes the possible cause of a problem, or reduces its probability.

Contingency action: provides stand-by arrangements to
offset or minimize the effects of a serious potential
problem.

The kinds of action taken in the cases described in this
chapter have not been specifically identified, in order that
the emphasis here may remain on the applications of the
concepts and methods of problem analysis, and not on the
choice of actions that necessarily follows decision making.

The facts of each of the cases we shall present have been
drawn from actual situations. In some cases, the results
were astounding, in others, the results were far better than
could be expected from ordinary hit-and-miss methods of
analysis. None of these cases are extra-special or highly
unusual. Some involved complete application of systematic
problem analysis to major, complex problems where managers carefully explored for relevant facts and distinctions
and changes, and verified their findings. Such applications
often produce spectacular savings in time and money.
However, complex, major problems are, after all, not a
daily occurrence; if they were, any company would soon go
out of business. So it is those less detailed applications,
often improvised to fit a particular need, that will perhaps
better illustrate the possibilities of using problem analysis
systematically, wherever the efficient use of information is
important—that is to say, practically everywhere in management. All these cases show how differently these concepts
and procedures have been applied by experienced managers who were not experienced in analyzing problems systematically. Many other examples could be cited, each
with its own variations and adaptations. But after reading

these cases the point should be clear: the proof of systematic problem analysis is in the application.

The importance of asking the right question in problem analysis has been demonstrated over and over again. Sometimes it is a question connected with the WHAT category of the specification, sometimes with the WHEN, sometimes with the WHERE. Here are some cases that illustrate how the questioning technique that systematically follows the specification procedure has uncovered hidden causes of problems in many different industries and companies:

Strike threat: An automotive company with six plants doing the same type operation was threatened with a strike involving personnel at a particular level of supervision. After asking many questions as to who was involved, what were the complaints, when did they start, and so on, the manager specifying the problem asked, "Where is the trouble occurring?" and was told the strike threatened all six plants. Then the manager asked, "Is it worse at some plants than at others?" This drew a surprised response, "Yes, it's worse at one plant than the other five." Then the manager asked "What is distinctive about that plant?" And, after a pause, the reply came, "By God, that one has *two* unions representing the same level of supervision!" This exposed the cause of the problem: a jurisdictional dispute that affected the five other plants which were not involved with actual grievances. The company changed its tactics and the strike threat evaporated.

Personnel evaluation: The top officials of one of the biggest banks in the U. S. were bothered by the poor performance of one branch manager. While all other branch managers had been achieving steady growth in deposits, new accounts, and volume handled, this manager hadn't. Apparently, many of his procedures, including his community relations efforts, were not effective. Nearly all the top officials agreed he should be replaced. Then one of them asked, "But do we really know what the cause of this problem is?" Some of his colleagues showed impatience with such a question, but he persisted and proposed that they specify the problem. When they put down the WHERE of this one branch and asked, "What might be distinctive of this location?" it came out that a couple of large companies had moved out of the area and loan values had fallen. Further checking revealed that the branch was in a dying industrial section. They checked with other banks in the area and found that their own branch was actually more successful; the manager was doing an outstanding job in the face of a locally declining economy. Result: they withdrew their decision to remove the manager and sent him a commendation.

Sales slow-down: An industrial products salesman covering one and a half Midwest states complained he could never stay on schedule in calling on dealers and users. He told his boss he might be off schedule by as much as a day or a day and a half at the end of a week-long trip. His planning methods, the priorities he set on calls, and his selling strategy seemed sound; his expectations as to what he should be able to do seemed realistic. His boss began systematically asking questions: "Was the salesman off schedule in the last three weeks?" Yes, he had been off the first, on the second, and off again in the third week. "How far off?" A day behind the first week, and a day and a half behind the third, but just right the second week. "What was distinctive about the first and third weeks?" This question revealed the fact that in those two bad weeks he had gotten phone calls from the regional sales manager asking him to check up on sales leads and complaints in the field. The changes in his itinerary and priorities upset his schedule; one week he had had to drive halfway across the state to attend to some relatively unimportant matter. The salesman's boss checked with other salesmen and found they were having similar trouble staying on schedule, and that none had realized that the regional manager's "help" was responsible. They thought they were to blame, and the regional manager himself was equally oblivious to the havoc his calls were producing. As soon as he stopped interrupting them, their scheduling improved.

Tool trouble: The purchasing manager of a multiplant company was having lunch with a plant manager to discuss some failures in cutting tools. As the plant manager described the way the tools had been burning up in use, the purchasing manager got "a mental image of the IS and the IS NOT of this problem," and realized that up to this point he had heard only about the IS. He asked some questions to fill in the IS NOT side of his mental specification: "Were the tools burning up at the Cleveland plant?" No, replied the plant manager. "Then what's distinctive about your operation as compared with Cleveland's cutting operation?" The plant manager thought a moment, then said, "Cleveland uses a water coolant, not oil." He suddenly realized he had found the cause of his problem in the use of oil as a coolant.

Case of the Bad Transistors

One of the most immediate on-the-job applications of some of the concepts and procedures of problem analysis occurred at a plant of one of the Big Three auto makers. At 9 A.M. one Monday morning, a chief engineer learned that one of the company's biggest customers had returned 90,000 transistors with a report that they were unusable. The chief engineer had just returned the previous Friday from a five-day training course in systematic analysis of problems and decisions, and he was eager to apply what he had learned. He immediately called in his top managers and asked them, "What's wrong?" They told him that the transistors were "no damn good." This was too general a reply for the chief engineer, who then insisted, "Yes, but what is wrong that makes them no damn good?" A few minutes later one of his men found that the transistors were failing through a breakdown in the paste solder used in them. But according to quality control, the transistors had passed inspection before they had been shipped and had gone bad later.

The chief engineer kept asking questions. "Did you have any trouble before this?" His men said they had had none. "Then what's different now? What have you changed?" The managers involved insisted that they had not changed anything, but the chief engineer refused to accept this. "You are getting failures now in the solder, and you didn't get them before, so you *must* have changed something. Go find out what it is." The men went back to their offices and did some more checking; pretty soon they were back with another story. "We did change something," they said, "we changed the cleaning flux used before the soldering, but the new flux is equal in all respects to the old flux." The chief engineer didn't believe it; he knew there had to be something wrong and he suspected the change to the new flux was the cause. "The hell it is the same," he said. "Go back and use the old flux. Also, find out what's eating up the solder in the new flux." The change back to the old flux corrected this transistor problem quickly, and laboratory tests later showed the cause of what was wrong with the new flux: a chemical in it left a residue in the metal and this, over a period of time, caused the paste solder to disintegrate and flake away. The transistors had been all right when they were completed and the solder was new, but by the time they reached the customer the solder had begun to go, and 90,000 of them soon tested out as rejects.

The chief engineer took about ten minutes all together to find the cause of this problem by asking a series of pertinent questions. Note that he did not stop to specify and analyze the problem in detail but as soon as he spotted a sharp IS and IS NOT contrast in the "when" category, he took a chance and jumped to his question about any possible changes that might have occurred. Fortunately, one change did provide the answer. If it had not, he would have had to back up and specify the problem completely and analyze it systematically for cause.

Case of the Plugged Spray Guns

But specifications of problems are not ordinarily as fast and simple as this. Sometimes the questions don't seem to lead anywhere at first, and persistence is required. Take

the "Case of the Plugged Spray Guns" reported by a manager in the Department of Streets of a large city in the U. S.
Street crews were busy the year-round, painting reflective
white and yellow center lines, crosswalks, safety zones, and
so forth, and one day the spray guns began plugging up.
The crews had to stop and clean the guns with paint thinner, then start up again, only to find the guns again plugging up. They blamed the design of the guns, the paint,
the weather, and each other. Finally the manager called
the superintendents of the crews into his office to specify
the problem. The WHAT and the WHERE were easy: the
guns were plugging up in the spray nozzles, and this was
happening with all crews, all over the city. But the WHEN
produced an argument. One man said, "Whenever we use
the guns." Another said, "No, only sometimes." After a lot
of probing questions, the manager found out that the
nozzles clogged when paint first began to go through them;
if they did not clog up immediately, they functioned per-
fectly until the next time the guns were used, usually the
next day. He said, "So they clog up in the morning." But
he was corrected: "No, no, they may clog up all day long,
but if they get unclogged, they stay unclogged for the rest
of the day." The manager tried again: "Then they clog up
at the start of the run and stay clogged until they are unclogged." This was not a very neat statement of the problem but it was the best they could do.

Then they began probing for distinctions. One man
said, "This sounds crazy, but the thing that's distinctive at
the start of the run is that the guns are *clean!*" The manager asked, "Do you change anything when you clean a

gun?" This scored the first break. "Well," one man said, "you wash the gun out with thinner and there's some thinner left in the gun afterwards." They decided they had better check the thinner. They put in some paint and saw it coagulate into small globules just large enough to plug a gun. Experimenting, they found that guns with thinner left in them clogged up immediately as paint entered the nozzle. But this now brought up a new puzzle: they had used the same paint and thinner for years, made to specifications set by the state highway department. They started phoning for more information, and found they were, indeed, using the same brand, but that the manufacturer had changed some of its ingredients, not realizing that the new mixture tended to clog in the presence of the thinner made by another manufacturer. A switch to another type of thinner solved the problem, just as smaller cities in the state were beginning to report the same trouble.

Case of the Veering Missiles

Some of the toughest problems for analysis crop up in the technical fields, such as missile research. One Navy research team, trained in systematic problem analysis, struggled hard to find out why an important new air-to-air missile sometimes went wild after being fired from high-speed jet interceptors. The missile would veer all over the sky and finally tumble end over end, endangering other aircraft and people on the ground. The research team had to work with scattered reports from a dozen different stations and ships; the speeds of the firing aircraft varied a great deal, and different types of craft were involved. The team found that most failures occurred at high altitudes, but some at low and medium altitudes. The missile always failed in the air, never in ground firings on the desert test range, so the team's specification of the problem was pretty sketchy.

Then a break came when a pilot reported his plane was hit by something shortly after a missile he had fired began to veer and wander. A long dent in the fuselage led to speculation that one of the missile's fins had come off and smacked into the plane. But no fin could be found in a search of the ground area below the accident, nor was enough left of the missile body, when it was recovered, to supply any useful information. However, a few days later a high-speed camera mounted on a jet interceptor caught pictures of a fin coming off a missle shortly after it was fired. The missile then began to veer and tumble end over end. So the cause of the problem of the veering missiles was at last identified, and without much help from systematic problem analysis.

But now the cause of this problem became itself a new problem, as we pointed out in discussing the "stair-step" procedure in Chapter 4. What made the fins come off? The research team began to specify this problem. Meanwhile the aerodynamics experts investigated the flutter characteristics of the fin in a high-speed wind tunnel, but they could not make a fin come off the missile. They couldn't even produce a serious flutter; the fin was excellently designed and securely held by bolts of high tensile strength that were threaded into the missile. The research team's specification, however, now began to reveal clues to the trouble.

A sharp contrast showed up between the IS and the IS NOT of the WHERE category: "in airborne operations," "not on the ground," and "at high altitudes mostly," "not at low altitudes." The team listed a number of conditions and factors that were distinctive of in-flight operations and high altitudes: vibration, reduced air pressure, high G-forces, and cold. Then they searched for changes in these distinctions and recognized the fact that in the distinctive condition "cold," metal contracted. So they began to speculate on possible causes related to such a change. "Suppose," they said, "that two different metals contracted at different rates and this allowed the fin to become loose?" They checked this out: the bolts were made of material with a high coefficient of expansion and contraction while the missile body, in which the bolt was threaded, was made of metal with relatively small expansion and contraction capacities.

The team had its answer: at the very low temperatures of high-altitude flight, the bolt "shrank" and became loose enough to pull free when the missle was fired. This was verified by examining a tap in one mis-fired missile body where the threads of the tap were stripped outward by the departing bolt. A complete verification of the team's analysis came when the failure of the fin was reproduced on the ground firing range by freezing the missile before launching. And a check of the recorded failures showed that in no case had a warm missile failed; where failures had occurred at medium and low altitudes, the firing aircraft had always descended after a period of high-altitude, sub-zero flight. So the team confidently recommended taking action to

deepen the tap in the missile body and use a weaker but
less contractive metal in the bolts. When these changes
were made, all missiles kept their fins and flew straight.

Case of the Holey Paper

Let us now examine a case where the problem was both
major and so very complicated that only the most complete
and careful specification and analysis uncovered the cause.
This "Case of the Holey Paper" occurred at the mill of a
papermaker, where, beginning in 1960, production problems, always imminent in so complicated a process, had
become critical for periods of several months during three
successive years. In the first crisis, the chief problem was
the appearance of holes in the paper sheet that produced
breaks in the finished rolls. This problem was tackled in a
"shotgun" manner; the supervisors assembled any and all
persons in the mill who might contribute to the situation,
and put them to work examining, analyzing, testing, and
doing anything or everything they could to find the cause
of the problem. The problem finally went away after ex-
tensive work was done on machine operating conditions.
But the following year another, similar crisis developed
with holes in the paper, and lasted for three months, during which the "shotgun" approach was again used. Eventually, adjustments were made that provided conclusive
evidence that ground-wood pitch had been the main cause
of the problem. But the following year the holes began
appearing again and another crisis developed, with the
supervisors again frantically working to locate the trouble.
This problem was now costing the company some $55,000

a month. And this time the plant manager himself became involved; he appointed a task force of five supervisors who were to devote their full time to concentrating on locating the cause through a systematic analysis of the problem.

The task force described the deviation as "excessive breaks in the sheet of paper due to pickout holes." The immediate technical cause of these holes was known: foreign matter, such as crumbs, drops of water, and pitch, formed lumps in the sheet, and holes then resulted when these lumps were scraped off by the blade of the paper coater at one point of the process. Not surprisingly, the first efforts of the task force to specify the problem were not too successful. A papermaking machine is really a series of machines and processes that stretch the length of a city block, and to gather information to specify this problem from this stretch of machines and processes would be a monumental task. Moreover, their job was terribly complicated by the fact that though much information was available, it was not the right kind and not precise enough. For example, there was no good description of exactly what "pickout" holes looked like, or when they became excessive in number, and there also was no exact information on what changes had occurred and when.

The task force decided to divide their job into two stages: (1) gathering specifying information; (2) getting information on possible causes. This cut down the work a good deal, but, even with this approach, it took the five men several days of intensive questioning and analyzing records before they could cull out the precise information that would describe the problem. The first specification they came up with looked like this:

	IS	IS NOT
WHAT	Breaks due to pickouts	Breaks due to other defects
WHERE	At second coater, treating wire side	At first coater, treating felt side
	In paper machine No. 1	No. 2 machine
WHEN	June to September, 1962, continuing June to September, 1960	Other times

From this specification the task force drew the following distinctions: (1) defect is in sheet; (2) breaks ordinarily are formed at first coater; (3) hundreds of distinctions between paper machines; (4) changes in temperature of the river water used during the summer. With such a loose specification, the number of possible causes appeared almost astronomical. Any experienced papermaker could describe literally hundreds of things distinctive of paper machine No. 1 as compared to No. 2, and there could be dozens of known changes in these distinctive areas. In short, the first step in analyzing this problem left such a wide area for possible causes that the task force realized it would have to sharpen its specification intensively. This took some discipline, since they might well have begun a "shotgun approach" to the problem at this point.

In respecifying the problem, the task force centered first on the point that these pickout holes in the paper usually occurred at the first coating machine and not at the second. They asked: "What was unusual about these pickout holes? Where do the pickout holes first appear in abnormal quantity?" Gathering this kind of information took a long time because most of it was not ordinarily available, and some of it was never available. But eventually, through the technique of asking questions, reading associated logs and reports, and discussing the situation in carefully planned conferences, the task force was able to present a very detailed statement of the problem.

The complications that developed in this specifying process are indicated by the fact that at one point the task force had developed these seven possible causes: (1) organization changes; (2) more defect-producing materials present; (3) pickability changed; (4) combination of cost, quality, and production pressure; (5) housekeeping; (6) seasonal changes; (7) insufficient alerts—not preventing problems. In analyzing its new specification, the task force had at last uncovered the fact that, although the break in the paper did not occur until the sheet had reached the second coating machine, the holes that allowed the breaks to occur showed up in the paper on the top side (felt side) before the sheet arrived at the first coating machine. This meant that the task force had to search for a distinction between the top side of the sheet and the bottom, or wire side, of the sheet. Looking for such a distinction would go against the grain of any experienced papermaker. All his experience tells him that the wire, or bottom side, of the sheet is the weakest side, and since this is the usual source of trouble, any search for cause should naturally be concentrated there. However, the task force persisted and realized that one part of the papermaking process distinctive of the top side, and occurring before the sheet reached the first coating machine, is the use of a big, polished granite roll that presses against a rubber roll and a felt blanket to squeeze out excess water from the sheet. A granite roll is used because its porous surface breaks the suction of this pressing process, and so releases the sheet. But here again papermaking experience was a handicap. For one thing, granite rolls are a much less likely source of trouble than nearly any other part of the papermaking process, and when they do cause trouble it is usually very easily identified. Moreover these pickout holes in the sheet did not look like granite-roll trouble at all to the eyes of these expert papermakers.

Nevertheless the task force pursued this distinction of the granite roll and looked for any changes connected with it. They knew that because the pores of a granite roll eventually become clogged, it is ordinarily changed every year or so on the machine. They found that this particular roll had been running about nine months but was not apparently generating the kind of usual trouble that would make it necessary to change it. However, at this point, one member of the task force, speculating on a possible cause, asked two questions: "Was the granite roll changed during that 1960 pickout crisis? Did the trouble go away immediately afterwards?" The answer to both these questions was yes. So the task force felt that the granite roll was the cause, and on their recommendation it was replaced. Result: The pickout holes practically disappeared and the $55,000 monthly loss was reduced to zero. Since then, the mill has been able to take effective action against the technical cause of this particular problem so that it has not reappeared.

A notable result of this problem analysis was that the mill undertook a drastic overhaul of its information-gathering systems. This provided better instructions and methods for gathering sharper specifying data for any problem an operator might see. A log of changes was set up that has since proved highly valuable in locating possible causes of plant problems. It is also notable that the task force completely documented its investigation and presented a report that covers more than fifty pages of specifying and analytical detail and graphs.

Case of the Crippled Motor

Other applications of systematic problem analysis show how effective this process can be when used by a group of managers possessing different specialties and experience. This showed up clearly at one large plant where the manager of engineering learned one Saturday morning, that a special 300-horsepower motor needed for daily production to meet a deadline had suddenly blown apart, while being installed by two of the electrical contractor's men. On hand also were nine other specialists; two representatives from the manufacturer of the electrical motor, three design-section electrical engineers, two maintenance engineers, an electrical foreman, and a master mechanic. Looking at the crippled equipment, all these managers assumed that the motor itself had failed and began jumping to various conclusions about the cause.

But the twelfth man, the manager of engineering, saw a chance here for an application of systematic problem analysis. He called the other men into his office and began putting questions to them, especially to the six who were electrical engineers. He wrote the facts he collected from them on a blackboard as he proceeded to specify the IS and the IS NOT of the problem. Drawing out the distinctions and then the changes, the engineering manager eventually listed four possible causes. As each new possible cause was put down, the group would adjourn briefly while some would go out and check the hypothesis on the spot. This system eliminated all but one possible cause: two of the circuit leads on the switchgear had been reversed and this had not been checked out when relocating the leads to the control panel, thereby "suiciding the generator volts to zero."

This cause was uncovered after about only a half hour of probing, and the motor was back in service the next Monday. By pinpointing this cause systematically, these managers had avoided tedious hours of work that would have been needed to check out all the circuits that conceivably might have caused the trouble. They also saved the company considerable sums in down time and lost production.

Case of the Stultified Staff Meetings

Let us now turn to the "Case of the Stultified Staff Meeting" and see how one group of managers is putting the concepts and procedures of problem analysis to work every single day. This example shows how problem analysis can become a continuous part of managerial thinking. This application took place in one division of a major company where the plant manager runs a twenty-four-hour, seven-day-week operation. For years this manager has been meeting with eight or nine of his key superintendents every weekday morning at 9 A.M. and sometimes on week-ends. The average length of these meetings was two hours; they should have taken far less time. Everybody involved agreed on two points: (1) the meetings were frustrating and time wasting, and (2) none of the managers could get along without them. One manager expressed the common complaint this way: "I sit there for two hours wishing I weren't there and thinking about all the things I have to get done. What I'm really waiting for are the two or three minutes of information that I have to have in order to stay out of trouble in my operation."

After the plant manager had been trained in systematic problem analysis, he took a long hard look at this meeting system and identified the problem as "too much time spent in meetings." He recognized that this problem could be broken into three parts, because the daily meeting performed three separate functions: (1) it was used to pass on general information; (2) it was used to report the current status of operations in each department; (3) and it was used to report and discuss particular problems such as the breakdown of equipment, unsatisfactory performance of men or groups, faulty manufacturing process, etc. Analyzing each separately, he saw no loss of time in the first function, since very little time was normally devoted to passing out general information. He saw that the second function (reporting on current status of operations) was redundant, and no time should be spent on this; he decided to eliminate this function entirely since such information was already available on a wall chart, which department heads could consult as they chose. Eliminating this function alone cut about twenty-five minutes off the average meeting time.

Now the plant manager concentrated on the third function of the staff meetings. He recognized his real problem was "too much time spent on reporting and discussing the hot problems in the plant." Too many problems, he realized, were being mixed together and talked about simultaneously, and there was too much complex analysis of a particular problem by two or three managers while the others sat around and waited. Then he recognized that there was a great deal of time spent in talking about possible causes and very little, if any, time devoted to specifying what the problems actually were. The plant manager was satisfied he had spotted the major cause of his lost-time problem, and he promptly made a decision. He established a new ground rule whereby the daily meetings would, henceforth, be used only to identify problems clearly, to set priorities, and to make assignments for working on specific problems or for reporting on problems previously assigned. Analysis of problems was strictly forbidden during the meeting.

Under this new rule, the meeting procedure calls for each superintendent to report the major current problems and potential problems in his area, and to identify each as to whether its cause is known or unknown. Each man also states whatever interim or corrective action may have already been taken on each problem. If the plant manager or his assistant or the division manager, who also lead these meetings, think that more details on a problem are needed, the superintendent involved will be asked to come into the plant manager's office after the meeting. A problem may be dropped with no further discussion if a superintendent says that the cause of a problem is known and corrective

	1	2	3	4	5	6	7
PROBLEM							
RESPONSIBILITY							
DATE RECOGNIZED							
INTERIM ACTION (if any)							
CAUSE AND DATE DETERMINED							
CORRECTIVE ACTION TAKEN AND DATE							
FOLLOW-UP: IS THE PROBLEM SOLVED?							

FIGURE 21 A major problem planning guide used to hold pertinent information on top problems at one company. This chart is printed on acetate so that information can be erased as priorities change and problems are solved.

action has been taken. But the plant manager, his assistant, and the division manager have all had training in systematic problem analysis, and they usually question the superintendents closely about "known" causes to find out to what extent the problem has been analyzed. If the cause of the problem is conceded to be unknown, the analysis of it is assigned and a report-back date is set. Sometimes the plant manager will set the priority at once by saying, "Let's take care of this immediately."

To help keep track of the problems and actions a chart was devised with room for only ten problems listed according to priorities. A sample of this chart appears in Figure 21. If more than ten problems are accumulated, those with the lowest priority are dropped from the list. The chart provides information under seven headings: the problem, responsibility, date recognized, interim action, cause, corrective action, and follow-up. This daily staff-meeting procedure has succeeded in cutting as much as an hour and a half from the time such meetings formerly consumed. The managers have, on the chart before them, the record of priorities and the assignments and actions to be taken, and thus they are not bothered with any elaborate system for handling these things. In addition, this procedure enables these managers to make visible to themselves the different things they may do in handling problems. They can keep separate the jobs of recognizing problems, specifying them, and finding cause; they see the differences between a general discussion of problems, and the analysis of problems; they can separate problems whose cause is known from problems whose cause is unknown; they are aware of the different purposes of interim action and corrective action. In short, these daily staff meetings now tend to impress on these managers the usefulness of building systematic problem analysis concepts and procedures into their own everyday thinking.

Case of the Scarred Faces

Now let us see how systematic problem analysis has been applied to some unusual puzzles. In the "Case of the Scarred Faces" it was a legal puzzle, and the task was to locate information that would identify an unknown. The manager here needed to apply only a few of the procedures described in this text, and he clearly demonstrated the advantages of a systematic method of searching out the relevant information, and doing so in a very short time. The case developed at 8:30 one morning when the manager of industrial security of one of the Big Three auto companies was asked to identify, by 4:30 that afternoon, two young girls with scarred faces whose photographs were handed to him, along with a group picture of them taken with their two brothers.

The picture was being distributed to members of a state legislature by lobbyists for dealers handling one type of safety glass used in automobiles. They were trying to show that it was dangerous to use a second type of safety glass which had been introduced by automobile manufacturers in car side windows. It was alleged that the young girls had been scarred in an accident by broken or flying glass of the second type. The legislature was about to vote on a bill that would have required the manufacturers to return to use of the original form of safety glass in the side windows of cars sold in that state. The automobile companies were concerned that the emotional impact of the distribution of the photos to legislators might insure passage of the bill to which they were opposed; they regarded the second form of glass at least as desirable from a safety standpoint as the first type.

The only specific information handed to the industrial security manager was that, according to the lobbyists, the scarred girls were sisters and had been injured in an automobile accident which was the subject of a law suit "somewhere other than the State of Illinois." The industrial security manager first divided his task into two parts: (1) find out who is the family in the picture, and (2) find out what happened to the scarred girls. Now note how he gathered and put together the needed information. Looking at the photographs of the girls, he made these two assumptions: (1) the family must reside in the North since the girls wore snowsuits; (2) the accident must have occurred long ago enough for the girls' faces to have healed with substantial scarred tissue. Obviously he needed more information. He decided then that this case appeared to involve the insurance function, the legal function, the medical function, and possibly the safety function in his company. His first step therefore was to ask the manager of each of these four departments to come to his office, study the photographs, and then help him find the identity of the family. He warned these managers not to begin looking for the cause of the scarred faces but to confine themselves to the search for the family's identity. Thus he intended to keep his specification of the facts free of conclusions about cause.

After examining the photographs, the head of the

medical department, a doctor, immediately concluded that the two individual photographs were of the same girl, showing different, advanced stages of recovery from the original wounds. The doctor also estimated it would have taken approximately eighteen months for these wounds to heal. This information nullified the lobbyists' statement that there were two girls involved. It also narrowed down the search; the eighteen-month healing period exceeded the period of time during which tempered glass had been used by two of the Big Three auto makers, which meant that the vehicle in the accident was made either by the other member of the Big Three or by a foreign car maker.

Armed with this information the manager of the legal department began phoning Company X (the other member of the Big Three) and the import distributors about a law suit involving a young girl. And the insurance manager similarly phoned several chief claims agents asking for any information or rumor concerning such a law suit. At 10:30 that morning a source in the insurance industry reported a rumor that this accident did actually involve Company X and that the claims amounted to $100,000. Another rumor that afternoon placed a case of this kind either in Buffalo, N.Y., or in a small community in Connecticut. A phone call to the director of safety for a large industrial company in the Connecticut town led to a local police officer who was able to review the accident in detail, including the fact that it was being handled by an independent New York law firm specializing in this type of claim. The police officer promised to send specific information on the name of the family, the date of the accident, and the police file numbers the following morning. This might have come too late, but fortunately word arrived at 4 P.M. that the legislature would not vote on the controversial safety glass bill until the next day.

Using the information he now had, the industrial security manager found out from Company X that it had identified the case, and that a representative of the New York law firm handling it was at Company X's headquarters and had files on the case with him. So within an hour the details of the accident, as reported by the investigating officer and witnesses, were in hand. This information indicated that the girl had been riding in the left-hand rear seat of a station wagon made by Company X, and since the scars were on the right-hand side of her face, there appeared little chance that these were caused by the window glass, as the lobbyists were claiming. Thus by 6 P.M. of that first day the manager seemed to have done remarkably well. He had identified the family and had some good evidence that the lobbyists had faked the photographs of the girl with the scarred face.

However, the wire that came in the next morning from the police officer in Connecticut added still more facts about the accident. One statement was that the accident had been reported to Cornell University Research Center, and the industrial security manager thought it was wise to follow up this tip. He shortly learned two important additional facts: (1) the back seat of the station wagon faced the rear, which therefore put the scarred side of the girl's face next to the window, a matter overlooked in the earlier reviews of the accident; (2) some glass particles from the accident had human tissue on them, which suggested a connection between the girl's wound and the glass. These two facts tended to reverse the confident assumption of the night before. It was apparent from all the facts that although the girl could have been cut by being hurled into the windshield, it was not possible to say conclusively that she had not been cut by broken side-window glass of the second type. Accordingly, the industrial security manager was able to advise his company's government affairs department not to challenge the validity of the photographs.

One other point about this case did not escape this investigating manager: relevant facts had been systematically uncovered by only three of the four other managers he had worked with. Though he had warned all four not to look for the cause of the girls' scarred faces but to concentrate on the identity of the family, one of the managers had been unable to resist looking for causes. By digging into the dispute between the glassmakers, this man managed to waste all the time he put in on this project.

Case of the Disappearing Meal

On some puzzling problems, where the cause remains invisible to expert eyes, systematic problem analysis has been used as a "direction finder" that locates the area where the cause should be looked for. A large soybean oil plant, for example, had been experiencing a strange shrinkage in soybean meal for several weeks, and it was decided, on the basis of some pretty general information, to check the hopper scales. These scales weigh the meal before it is bulk-loaded into box cars, and because several recent changes had been made on the scales, the investigators suspected them. First the plant superintendent checked the scales, then government inspectors checked them, and after several days of this work the suspicions evaporated: the scales were completely accurate. So the investigators stopped looking in the loading area for the cause of the shrinkage and began exploring plant operations. But very shortly a new puzzle appeared. A customer phoned and asked when the plant was going to bill him for the additional 4,000 pounds of meal he had received in the last box car sent to him. "What additional 4,000 pounds of meal?" the astonished superintendent asked. But the customer wasn't kidding; he had indeed received an overshipment, and a spot check revealed that other customers had been getting more than they'd ordered.

Shortly after this discovery four managers—the superintendent, two foremen and the traffic manager—began systematically to specify the problem of the shrinking meal. They had just spent a week studying systematic problem analysis, and one of the first questions they asked about WHERE turned up the fact that the overloading was occurring only on shipments originating on the east spur of the loading conveyor, but not on the west spur shipments. This contrast immediately eliminated the scales as the culprit, since the same scales were used on both spurs of the conveyor. All the time spent checking the scales had obviously been pointless. Also, since the specification indicated that the overloading was taking place on every shift, human errors were eliminated as possible causes. Then when they looked for distinctions, the only relevant one they found was in the WHERE dimension: there was an additional unused short spout coming off the east conveyor. Had there been any change in this spout? The managers at once went out and examined it. Yes, the spout had been blocked off by a metal plate that had trapped water and rusted through leaving a sizable hole. The hole in the blocking plate was the change. Now in a matter of moments they had found the change that was the cause of their puzzling problem: on its way to the scales some of the meal would drop through this rusty hole into the box car and so remain unaccounted for, a free contribution to the customer.

Case of the Inhibited Customers

The usual analysis of marketing problems is often as hit-and-miss as the analysis of production problems. But in the following "Case of the Inhibited Customers" the procedures of systematic problem analysis were ingeniously applied to a sales problem by a manager in one of the big pharmaceutical companies. In this case, he applied these analysis procedures to the main difficulties salesmen encountered in selling big accounts, including hospitals, laboratories, and state institutions. He saw that salesmen needed to handle a great deal of information about each customer, but that salesmen rarely approached a customer with a specific idea as to how much he wanted to sell to the customer. When a customer didn't place an order the salesmen usually blamed this on price or competition, and they also repeatedly used the same sales approaches on successive calls until they finally gave up. These tactics, the manager concluded, had obscured the real sales problem. Salesmen were looking at the wrong possible causes to explain the lack of sales. The manager saw the problem very differently. The "should," as he saw it, was selling 100 per cent

of the market; he made the bold assumption that *every* sale
could be made, even when the company held 85 per cent
of the market. He saw three possible causes for any deviation from this high performance standard: (1) poor salesmen; (2) poor products; (3) customer inhibited from
buying by other factors. He dismissed the first and second
possible causes on the basis of other evidence, for he rated
his company's salesmen as equal to the best, and he knew
his company did not market any product unless it was a
contribution to medicine and was considered superior to
anything else then being used. Thus the third possible
cause of the problem, inhibited customers, became the
most likely cause, and, by the stair-stepping process, it also
became a problem to be analyzed for cause. He stated
the problem in this way: "Customer X is inhibited from
buying from our company."

To find the cause of this problem, the manager reasoned
that it would be necessary to find out what distinguished
each customer from all other customers. The salesman's
task in each case would always be to locate the factor or
factors that had inhibited a sale to this customer, and then
to "zero in" on this obstacle. The manager decided that
the salesman could adapt some problem analysis techniques to this task, finding the contrasts between what they
expected to happen in a sales conference and what did
happen, between what they expected to present to the customer and what they actually presented, and between what
they expected the customer's reaction to be and what these
reactions really turned out to be. The manager also recognized the need to explore many of the informal and personal relationships of the actual buyer; this would include

his status in the company, his control over purchasing, his influence on others, and also his personal biases that might block a sale.

To collect this kind of information the manager thought that two "agendas" could be devised. One would be a running account of each sales prospect, including biographical data, professional associations, levels of authority, etc. This data would be modified by the salesmen after each call, when he had analyzed the distinctive factors he had found in each case. The other agenda would be a written outline of what to discuss with the customer when selling, i.e., a program of what the customer might buy in the light of the information gathered from the biographical data and other information. So a series of questions was developed for the salesmen to answer about each customer. The salesmen were provided with basic biographical data on all customers and prospects, and also given data about specific hospital practices, tests, quantities of chemicals used, etc. The salesmen could then use this information in assessing accurately each particular customer's needs. As finally developed, the "agenda presentations" now cover some fourteen different points that salesmen are expected to explore in connection with every customer.

The research done on a particular customer may take considerable time. In one case the salesman spent sixteen months trying to sell a director of a large laboratory. He had good rapport with this man and had convinced him, logically, that the quality of his company's product was superior to others. But the lab director continued to hold back. So the salesman built up "agendas" on nearly a dozen other people in the laboratory who were in a position to influence the director in his purchases. Finally the salesman located the "inhibitor," a young British doctoral student who turned out to be the last man in the chain of command reporting to the director. This technician had been schooled in using traditional products and methods, and his somewhat aggressive manner had great influence with the director who was inclined to be "passive" and conservative in his purchases for the laboratory. Once the salesman had indentified this technician as the sales "inhibitor," he called on him and found out why he had objected to his company's product. Then he proceeded to sell him on the advantages of using these same products. Shortly thereafter the salesman successfully sold the director on buying his company's products for the laboratory.

Only about 15 per cent of the inhibited customers turn out to be complex cases for analysis. Usually the key purchaser can be persuaded after "agendas" have been developed on a few of the customer's top men. The larger the hospital or medical school or institution, the more complex the situation, and in state institutions it may be especially difficult to find the particular "inhibitor" who blocks the sale. But once the salesman has identified the specific distinctions between customers, he can see why previous approaches have been unsuccessful and how the sales situation should now be handled. Moreover, the "agendas" provide a continuous help, for whenever a purchaser or a potential "inhibitor" moves to another location, the data on him is forwarded to the salesmen in the new territory. The company has now developed "agendas" covering "satellite people" to be found around the major purchasers of their products. Many of the salesmen have said, "It's the only way to sell—why haven't I thought of it before?" As for the customer, he gets the benefit of having the salesman think through the customer's particular needs, so he can supply him intelligently.

USEFUL TECHNIQUES

One of the most difficult steps in problem analysis is backtracking to locate the change that produced an effect that later took on the status of a problem. The change may be unrecognized as such, or forgotten, or not seen as relevant; it may be buried in data that accumulates daily. Yet at one point or another, the change has undoubtedly been seen by someone. Managers who have been trained in systematic problem analysis have developed various ways of dealing with this difficulty of tracking down hidden or buried changes. Here are some of these practical techniques:

A Log for Recording Change

Managers of one of the largest computer firms, appalled at the number of production changes that take place every day about which they receive no first-hand information, use a log to record changes in the manufacturing line. In this log each change made or observed is set down, with the time and date and the name of the person making the entry. When things go wrong, the log is consulted at once for changes that might point to possible causes. As indicated earlier, a similar log is maintained by a major paper company on its production line, and an electronics manufacturer has adopted a system of posting a card before each operator and assembler who is instructed to record any change he observes right when it occurs. This system speeds up problem analysis; for example, one entry, "First batch of transistor caps from X Company," recorded a change from one supplier to another, and this one change provided a fast solution to a quality problem that otherwise might have taken days or weeks to clear up.

Logs of this kind may be especially useful in laboratory work. For example, the manager of the photographic section at a Navy missile test station keeps a log of changes in his lab, in processing methods, in equipment, solutions, and so forth. Even minute changes may have major unexpected results, for the lab uses colorimetric and spectroscopic examination of extremely precise slow-motion color photography in measuring the temperature of missile engine firings. When trouble emerges, the manager finds it easy to go back to the log and scan it for any changes that may have occurred within an area of distinction. Formerly, such changes went unrecorded.

A Map of Problem Analysis

The chart or plastic card, showing the "wheel" of concepts illustrated in Figure 9 on pages 54–55, is often used as a map to guide managers in locating themselves in dealing with a problem. The assistant plant manager of a major aircraft company has taped this chart to the sliding writing panel of his desk, and pulls it out when a problem comes up, to review where *he* is in the process of analyzing the trouble, or of analyzing a decision about it. Another manager has placed copies of the "wheel" under the glass top of his conference table where those participating in meetings can easily see it. From time to time he asks them, "Where are we on the wheel? Is this a problem or a decision?"

For a great many managers this diagram of concepts is particularly useful in coaching their subordinates. When discussing a situation these managers use it to point out the kind of information that is needed to analyze a problem or a decision. For example, a manager might show a subordinate that he has to find out more about the WHERE and the WHEN of a problem before he can begin to analyze it for the distinctive factors that will lead him to the change that caused it. Also, by referring to the "wheel" of concepts, managers coach their subordinates in the kinds of questions they should be using—and the systematic order of questioning—in getting information on a problem or a decision.

A Guide for Making Recommendations

The conceptual scheme presented in Chapter 3 has been effectively used as an outline for making recommendations to superiors. The city manager of a large city on the west coast, for example, has adopted this outline in reporting to his board of trustees. He has found that a good report must include: (1) what was expected by the trustees, or what should be happening; (2) what is actually wrong and a precise description of it; (3) what is distinctive of the problem; (4) what has changed; (5) possible causes that have been tested; (6) the basis for the determination of the cause.

With this foundation of information, the city manager's recommendations for action are, he finds, more understandable to the trustees. His reports have been accepted without opposition much more often than they were before he applied this guide based on the concepts of problem analysis and decision analysis. Others have used such a guide for their recommendations even more successfully; a top administrator in one of the largest federal agencies, for example, reports as follows: "It never misses. When my superior sees all the information I've laid out for him in this way, he understands both the problem and why I've suggested the action on it that I have."

A Recording Form

Information about problems sometimes comes so fast and often that a lot of it gets lost before it can be used. An executive in one of the largest insurance companies continually receives reports on a wide range of problems in the field, and he is expected to act on these quickly. He has devised the form shown in Figure 22 for gathering preliminary information over the phone, gauging the severity of each problem, and deciding whether to ignore it or assign it to someone for follow-up. The form gives him a means of handling all this information systematically. It provides him with a record of each of the many problems he is involved with every day; it gives him a tangible body of information to pass on to those subordinates to whom he delegates the follow-up. And the subordinates themselves have an organized platform from which to move into the analysis and solution of each problem.

Finally, this chapter on the applications of systematic problem analysis may be usefully concluded by describing

Date _____

Telephone call /___/ From /___/ To _____ Ext. _____
Policyholder: _____
Policy No. _____ Priority _____
Situation:

Decision:_____ to do Follow-up on _____

IS	IS NOT	DISTINCTIONS
WHAT:		
WHERE:		
WHEN:		
SIZE:		

Reverse side for KNOWN CHANGES, POSSIBLE CAUSES, TEST, VERIFICATION.

FIGURE 22   A recording form used by an executive in a large insurance company when getting down information on problems as it comes to him over the phone from his people in the field. The reverse side is used for recording information on "known changes," "possible causes," "test," and "verification."

how such analysis led two managers to some unexpected conclusions about their own performances. In this "Case of the Surprised Managers," a regional manager and an executive manager of a large insurance adjustment firm discovered that within a seven-month period five out of a total staff of ten casualty adjustors had resigned, and the turnover was growing even worse. Both managers attributed the resignations to four causes that they had long assumed responsible for turnover: (1) casualty men are natural drifters; (2) casualty men will change jobs just to get a $25-a-month raise; (3) the company didn't have the variety of casualty claims that would hold and challenge good casualty men; (4) the company's salary schedule didn't attract good men with four to five years of experience. These causes were often cited as "hazards of the business" and the regional manager had become expert in putting together different combinations of these explanations when accounting for resignations from the staff. However, after both managers had studied systematic problem analysis they discussed this problem of resignations quite differently when they decided to analyze it for cause.

The problem was first recognized as one of "casualty staff resigning." Some exit interviews revealed that three of these casualty men had left because they had not been appointed district casualty supervisor, and two others felt there was no future in this company for them. But these explanations did not satisfy the two managers now. After some discussion they decided they had a new problem, which they stated this way: "General unrest in the casualty ranks within the state." The managers then specified this problem completely, and their analysis of the specification produced a number of distinctions and changes. These included: "Nonrecognition of accomplishment (managers and supervisors have been recognized for their accomplishments whereas the adjustors have not been recognized)"; "casualty people still feel segregated from fire people"; "some casualty people have 'crown prince' attitudes"; "four-to six-year men are expecting recognition about this time of their career"; "adjustors want their vacation"; "adjustors not advised of changes in advance (managers and supervisors generally are in the know more than adjustors)."

From their analysis the two managers derived four possible causes: (1) failure to properly counsel with adjustors and advise them of changes that will affect them; (2) company may have created feeling that casualty people are "special people" and deserve special handling; (3) failure to recognize good work and give credit when due; (4) supervision is not good. But after testing these four possible causes against their specification the managers decided that these really added up to one most likely cause which they described this way: "Company policy toward the handling of people has been poor, and we have had inadequate supervision in the region." In short, the managers had to conclude from their analysis that the kind of management for which they themselves were responsible was the cause of the problem they were trying to solve. As the regional manager put it, "After this analysis of the problem, both the executive manager and I became aware that the cause was probably poor supervision, and this had never entered our minds before actually sitting down to specify the problem."

Now the two managers, facing the fact, systematically set out to decide what should be done about the problem. They followed the basic concepts and procedures of decision analysis, and the program that resulted has produced spectacular improvements. During the first eight months of the program, for example, the staff of casualty adjustors was increased from ten to seventeen men, yet only one resigned, and in this same period the total turnover of the whole staff dropped to less than 4 per cent. Such results could not have been expected had not the two managers first corrected their original assumptions about the cause of the high turnover problem, then made a very careful analysis of their decision, chosen the best corrective action, and finally implemented and protected this action by careful forethought about consequences and future problems. The concepts and procedures of decision analysis which these managers followed will be discussed in detail in the following chapter.

CAUSE DETERMINED

DECISION STATEMENT

ESTABLISH OBJECTIVES

- Results to be produced
- Resources to be used

CLASSIFY OBJECTIVES

STANDARD OF MEASUREMENT
RELATE JUDGMEST

MUSTS: Limits
WANTS: Weights

**GENERATE
ALTERNATIVE
COURSES OF ACTIONS**

COMPARE AND CHOOSE

MUSTS: GO/NO GO
WANTS: Relative fit

**ASSESS ADVERSE
CONSEQUENCES**

- Minimize threat

DECISION MADE

FIGURE 23 Decision making is the process of choosing between various
ways of getting a job done. This involves first the development of a standard of comparison, which is the list of objectives to be achieved by the
action contemplated. Against this standard each alternative is measured,
and one is chosen according to the manager's best judgment. Before acting
on this choice, he looks for possible adverse consequences, balancing advantages against disadvantages. A systematic decision is the product of a
great many small judgments, organized and summarized.

CHAPTER 10

Decision Analysis

Decision making is undoubtedly the most difficult and most essential task a manager performs. One kind of decision he makes is not connected with problems; he may decide to take an action that will set entirely new standards of performance, or will attain some new goal or establish a new direction for his company's operations. Decisions of this kind are extremely important but relatively rare. Usually, the manager is making decisions connected with problems, present or future, and many of the difficulties are eliminated, as we have seen, when he has mastered problem analysis and can recognize and specify problems and determine their causes accurately. Correcting a cause, however, calls for a different kind of analysis, an analysis that will provide a sound basis for choosing the best action that can be taken to correct the problem. A decision, as we previously pointed out, is always a choice between various ways of getting a particular thing done or an end accomplished. Making such a choice is often difficult, because a decision can be made only when a great many separate judgments have been made, derived from the examination of many facts. Most likely, a decision will be a compromise between what the manager wants, in an ideal sense, and what can actually be done. But his responsibility is to select that action that gets the most done, at the least cost and with the least disadvantages.

How does a manager do this? Many of the decisions that he faces in everyday operations involve very simple choices and relatively small amounts of information. He knows what his objectives are, he weighs their importance and assesses ways of doing a job, all in a matter of moments and without bothering to write anything down. This is quite appropriate. But when major decisions arise, and he is faced with a large amount of complicated information, he often does not bother to put down and assess all the factors involved. This is a mistake, for no manager is able to hold in his head all the various assessments and factors that may go into making a major decision. The process of decision making is difficult because it involves not only experience, knowledge, common sense, and judgment, but also a great many future uncertainties that may threaten the action decided upon. A systematic approach to decision making is therefore just as valuable as a systematic approach to problem analysis. Its value is in direct proportion to the increasing complexity of the task.

Before getting into the processes of decision analysis, let us look again at the kinds of actions a manager can choose in dealing with a problem. As we pointed out in the last chapter, there are five such kinds of action: interim, adaptive, corrective, preventive, and contingency. The last two will be taken up in the following chapter when we discuss potential problem analysis. Here we will be primarily concerned with those three actions—interim, adaptive, and corrective—that can be taken in dealing with current problems. If a manager does not recognize the differences between these three kinds of action, he is likely to find himself in trouble. A lot of managers, for example, often confuse interim action with corrective action, and confidently tell themselves, "Well, we've done something, and the problem has gone away. We won't have to worry about that again." But when the old problem reappears the manager will be much worse off than before. He will have lost a great deal of time, wasted resources, and confused the issue. Besides, by then others will know he didn't handle the problem right in the first place.

Each of the three possible actions on a current problem serves its own purposes and each is quite different. Let us consider each of them more specifically:

Interim action: This is usually the first kind of action taken, and it is taken before the cause has been found and corrective action becomes possible. Interim action is taken when the manager has to do something to keep the operation going. It is action that gives the manager time to complete specification and analysis of the problem to find the cause. This is stopgap action, and it may be very expensive, but it usually has to be taken if the problem is really serious. In the Butterfat Case described in Chapter 8, the vice president took an interim action by suspending all shipments to the complaining customer until he had nailed down the cause of the bad butterfat. Similarly, in the Black Filament Case described in Chapter 2, the manager could have reduced the rate of production as much as possible, while the problem was being analyzed. He also could have called in more technical help from the company's central laboratories. These would be stopgap actions, alerting others to the problem, collecting additional resources, and giving the manager time in which he could specify the problem and analyze it completely for cause.

Adaptive action: This is the kind of action a manager can take after he has located the cause of a problem and either finds he can't do anything to eliminate the cause, or decides that action to directly correct the deviation is not feasible. Adaptive action enables him to live with the effects of a problem and to minimize them. In some cases, this may be much more economical than corrective action. Adaptive action is sometimes all that a manager can take in situations where the cause of a problem lies outside his area of influence or control. In the Black Filament Case, the manager might have decided he wouldn't try to prevent the carbon from coming into the air intakes, but would arrange to have a wiping mechanism installed to clean off the carbon before the filament went into the buckets. This would be truly adaptive action: taking this action in full knowledge of what the cause was, but choosing this action rather than incur the expense of an air-filter system.

Corrective action: This is the action that eliminates the deviation by eliminating the cause that produced the problem. As a general rule, the most efficient action is corrective action. But it is only possible where the cause is known. The vice president in the Butterfat Case took corrective actions when he knew the cause of the putrid butterfat, and so had the takeoff temperature reduced and the palletizing procedure changed. The other actions he took, such as making sure quality control standards were understood, authorizing overtime, ordering a test to verify the changes, were taken to prevent future problems. In the Black Filament Case, one corrective action could have been simply for the manager to order that under no circumstances should the switching engine stop near the air intakes of the plant, but should be parked across the tracks by the water tower, if the train crew wanted to stop in for a late cup of coffee. Or he might have requested that a nonsmoking diesel switch engine be used in the yards. Either action would have been cheap and would have removed the cause.

On many problems it is frequently necessary to take, successively, both interim and corrective actions. This was done in the case of the Lockheed Electra airplanes that came apart at high altitudes and crashed in the early 1960s. The FAA and the CAB first took interim action by reassuring the public, announcing that they were studying the problem, gathering information on it, and trying to find the cause of the crashes as quickly as possible. These announcements, of course, did nothing about the cause, but they did give the agencies time to find out what was really happening to these planes.

Next, the head of the FAA at that time, General Quesada, took a second and very courageous interim action. Though he still did not know the cause, he refused to ground the planes, as many were asking him to in the belief that the Electra was an unsafe aircraft. Because he was convinced it was a well-built airplane, he ordered the maximum cruising speed of the plane reduced sharply. By this interim action, the FAA aimed to reduce the risk of another failure, and buy time in which to carry out an analysis. The action was, in effect, saying: "There's something wrong with the aircraft that makes it break up. We don't know what it is, but if we fly slower, the plane probably won't break up."

Having gained time by these two interim actions, the FAA and CAB worked rapidly to locate the cause of the Electra crashes. They found that the wings had been torn out of the fuselage by a combination of two things: a particular flutter in the outer wing panel and an oscillation of the nacelle of the outboard engine. These two vibrations augmented each other to produce a "harmonic" with enough force to rip the wing off. Once this cause was determined, the two agencies could at last take corrective action to eliminate it: they had the manufacturer stiffen the nacelles, and modify the wings to reduce flutter, so as to prevent the reoccurrence of the deadly "harmonic." As part of the corrective action, the manufacturer also voluntarily installed (at a cost of almost $30 million) some 1,800 pounds of added steel spars in the wings, so that if vibration did start, the wing would be too stiff to allow it to develop to a dangerous degree.

The times when it is not possible to take any action that will eliminate the cause of a problem are common in the case of catastrophes caused by natural forces. Only adaptive actions can then be taken. The Alaskan earthquakes in 1964, for instance, produced a major problem of public safety, but corrective action, such as devising some mechanism or technique that would remove the cause of the earthquake, was clearly impossible. In industry, too, there are sometimes major problems for which corrective actions cannot be found. One example occurred in 1964 after California ruled that by 1966 new automobiles in the state would have to be equipped with exhaust control systems that would reduce air pollution. The major auto companies were not expected to supply such equipment before 1967, but General Motors unexpectedly announced it would be able to equip 95 per cent of its 1966 models with exhaust control devices, and the other big auto makers soon also began tooling up to equip their 1966 models with such devices. The result was that half-a-dozen independent manufacturers of exhaust control systems suddenly faced the complete loss of the big market they had been counting on, and there was no corrective action they could take that would get rid of the cause of their problem.

In any case, whatever action a manager chooses to take will involve decision making. And any decision as to whether to take interim, adaptive, or corrective action against a problem should be systematically developed by following the seven basic concepts of decision making described in Chapter 3. These seven concepts involve a number of different procedures, which we will consider under seven separate phases, as follows:

1. Setting objectives against which to choose
2. Classifying objectives as to importance
3. Developing alternatives from which to choose
4. Evaluating alternatives against the objectives to make a choice
5. Choosing the best alternative as a tentative decision
6. Assessing adverse consequences from the choice
7. Controlling effects of the final decision

The logic behind this sequence of actions is clear enough. Setting objectives lays the groundwork for a decision. You cannot choose the best way of getting somewhere until you have determined where you want to end up, specifically. That means you have to define your objectives in detail; what it is that you are trying to get done, and just what degree of emphasis you put on each part of the job.

With this yardstick as a guide, you can then develop several alternative ways of getting the job done, accepted ways as well as entirely new ways. Then you can measure each one of these alternatives carefully, point by point, against the criteria laid down in the objectives. This puts you in a position to make a tentative choice of that alternative which looks like it will do the job best. To make sure it is the best, you explore this alternative for any future troubles it might produce, and the adverse consequences attached to it. Finally you control the decision you have made by taking the action necessary to prevent these adverse consequences from occurring, and you follow up to see that the course of action decided on is carried out.

This process of decision making is a systematic putting together of facts and experience to produce a better judgment on the part of the manager. It is the organization of the relevant information into a form that can be clearly understood and handled in the making of a choice. In a way parallel to the process of problem analysis, it is the manipulation of information so that a series of needed comparisons can be made.

This process also corrects common errors in decision making. One of these errors occurs, for example, when managers search first for alternatives and then begin to evaluate these without stopping to set the objectives of their actions. Then they commit another error by proceeding to choose the alternative and letting this alternative set their objectives. Thus a new product may be chosen from among several candidates, and the nature of this product then, in effect, sets the market objectives of the company. Another danger in jumping into the search for alternatives without first setting out the objectives is that implicit objectives may limit the search; for example, implicit ideas about the business the company is in can seriously limit the range of alternate projects considered by the company's research staff.

Obviously it makes little sense for a manager to try to pick the best of several possible courses of action if the job it has to do has not been defined. On the other hand, if objectives have been clearly set out, he knows what he is looking for when he starts the search for alternatives. He has a list of particulars that takes him more directly to his target. And he also has a way of evaluating these alternatives once he has found them. Many managers gather a wealth of detail about possible courses of action but have no systematic procedure for using that information fully in making the end decision.

The methods outlined in this chapter will not assure a manager of successful decision making. No method can do that. But this procedure should help him capitalize on his experience and the facts available, so as to make a good judgment. After all, he is going to have to make the decision anyway. The more systematically he can go about it, the more chance he has of bringing his experience and good judgment to bear.

Now let us look at each of the seven stages in this decision-making process and see how they relate to each other and contribute to the improvement of decision making:

1. *Establish objectives.*

This step, extremely important, is often omitted or superficially done, in decision making. Often only the broad idea of the objective is stated, such as "make more profit." Such an objective is too vague to be of much use as a standard of comparison in choosing between ways of doing business. The objective must be specified. *What* kind of profit? *How much? When* and *where?* The objective should describe the goal precisely and locate it in time, place, and number. Thus "make more profit" becomes "make 10 per cent net profit after taxes in this accounting year." This gives a standard which states how much, how it is to be figured, and within which time period it should fall. This is a standard that can be used as a yardstick in assessing the facts available to a manager about any alternative. With this kind of an objective, he can determine that a proposed action does or does not produce a particular return, or how close it comes to the goal.

Objectives are derived from two general areas: the *results* expected to come from a decision, and the *resources* available for expenditure in carrying out a decision. Every decision is a transaction of this sort: a manager uses some of his resources to get something done. The objectives that he sets are his guidelines in the use of resources and the gaining of advantageous results and returns.

The manager usually starts with the results he expects to achieve. To determine these, he questions his knowledge and solicits information. He asks: What is to be accomplished? What problems are we trying to correct? What situations are we trying to improve? Where are we trying to go? What returns do we want for our effort? What functions are to be performed to get there? What kinds of things are to be avoided, if at all possible? What kinds of results do we want to minimize?

Similarly, in seeking information about resources to be committed, the manager explores the following areas:

Men—skills, numbers

Money—capital, budget, cost

Material—facilities, equipment, space

Time—short term, long term

Power—energy, transport, authority

Using this list of resources as a guide, the manager asks: What are the resource limits within which I must stay? What is available? What must be conserved? What should be utilized? What use of resources should be minimized? What use of resources should be maximized?

The answers to these questions about results and resources will give the manager the objectives he wants his decision to accomplish.

2. *Classify objectives according to importance.*

All the objectives that have been listed will assert some degree of influence on the course of action that is selected. But some will be of absolute and overriding importance, some will be quite important but not mandatory, others will be nice to accomplish as a bonus but probably won't affect the situation a great deal, one way or another. All the objectives should be listed under two headings: MUSTS and WANTS. The MUSTS set the limits that cannot be violated by any alternatives. If a new product must be on the market with a capital outlay of no more than $200,000, and a new idea comes along that would require twice that amount, this new idea can't be touched no matter how intriguing it is. It is beyond the dollar limits that have been set as a MUST. Similarly, there may be a result that is absolutely required if the decision is to be a success. Maximum and minimum limits should be set for both critical resources and required results. These

MUST objectives help the manager to recognize and screen out the impossible alternatives right at the outset.

Objectives that are WANTS do not set absolute limits but express relative desirability. For instance, a manager would like to spend *less* of his resources than the maximum limit he has set; he would like to produce *more* results and returns than the minimum requirements set; he will want to avoid legal entanglements or continuing expense on an item. These WANT objectives are concerned with relative advantage and disadvantage.

By distinguishing between MUSTS and WANTS in setting objectives, the manager avoids the mistake of

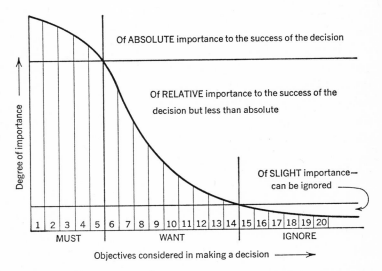

FIGURE 24 This chart shows that objectives relevant to the success of a decision are of declining importance. Reading from left to right, MUST objectives have a GO/NO GO effect on the decision, WANT objectives carry successively less and less weight, and inconsequential factors can safely be ignored.

settling for an alternative action, only to find later that it isn't satisfactory because he forgot some essential require-ment in making his decision. On the other hand, if he does separate the MUSTS and the WANTS, the manager may find that none of the alternatives he has developed are satisfactory, and he will thus be impelled to go on looking for better alternatives. At the same time, the separation of MUSTS and WANTS enables the manager to reach the best alternative more efficiently, since the MUSTS screen out all the poorer alternatives.

The decision-making manager will find that some WANT objectives will always be far more important, more critical than others, and here he has to sharpen his judgment as to the degree of their relative importance. To do this he has to weigh each one carefully.

The first step in this weighing process is to establish the position of each WANT objective with relation to the next. This is done by giving it a numerical weight of importance. Such weighting can be done by starting with the least important objective and giving it a weight of 1, then asking how many times more important another ob-jective is compared to it, and giving this second objective a weight in accordance, say 3 or 5. Then each of the re-maining objectives can be treated the same way. By this method the least important objective is taken as a bedrock standard of comparison, and all other objectives are ranged against it. Another method is to use a straight numerical scale, say from 1 to 10. The particular scale used is not critical, but it should have sufficient spread to allow for discrimination in recording the importance of each objec-tive in relation to the others. The manager's judgment as to the weight of each WANT objective is drawn from his own experience and from the experience of others. What is critical is that some assessment of relative importance be made.

3. *Develop alternatives from which to choose.*

The set of MUST and WANT objectives becomes a set of specifications by which to develop alternative courses of action. The objectives spelled out are individual statements of functions to be performed or fulfilled by the course of action. Once a manager has set out the functions that must be performed, and the functions he wants to have performed, and has indicated how important he thinks these WANTS are, one compared to another, he already has the basic dimensions and requirements in hand for establishing the alternatives. He has a blueprint of what it is he must build. Now all he has to do is fill in the details.

To do this, a manager reaches into his experience and fund of knowledge for the components with which to build a coherent whole. He examines each objective by itself. He asks: What kind of things does this imply? What are the various actions that might supply this requirement? What do I know about this or what means have others used to fill a similar need? He puts these together as a collection of the best ways he knows of meeting the individual objectives. Now he must put these best ways together into a feasible, total course of action, or alternative. Each step he takes is calculated and rational, based upon the analysis he has made of the job to be done.

Some of the alternatives he develops will be ready-made, off-the-shelf items. For example, the ready-made alternative might be the acquisition of a unit of capital equipment where several makes or models might do the job, but one will do it better than the others. Or the choice might be between two products or components, or between candidates for a particular position. Other alternatives must be generated from scratch, literally invented. Such alternative courses of action would be the development of a new sales campaign, or a new organization, or a new product, or a new job and set of responsibilities and authorities.

Finding alternatives is not a hit-or-miss affair, but a patient, careful search for a specific action that will perform a certain precise function. After all, a manager is only looking for one course of action, the best according to the standards he has set. The more systematically he uses those standards in searching, the more efficiently he can move through a number of possibilities to find the best action.

4. *Evaluate the alternatives against the objectives to make a choice.*

To evaluate an alternative, the manager tests it against the objectives, measuring it to see how good a job it will do. He is interested in the performance of things, and he has stated the performance he is after in his objectives. His assessment will be made up of a great many separate judgments, derived from his examination of many facts. To do this systematically, he takes each alternative and measures it individually against each one of the MUST and WANT objectives separately. Each alternative is first assessed against the MUST objectives on a GO/NO GO basis. If an alternative fails to perform what a MUST objective requires, it must be immediately discarded. The MUST objectives will screen out the impossibilities and reduce the number of possible alternatives to the relevant few. Alternatives that satisfy all the MUST objectives can then be evaluated further against the WANT objectives.

For some MUST objectives it is important to evaluate the degree to which the alternatives exceed the minimum. For example, if a MUST objective of a decision is to net $100,000 profit in the first year, the alternative that nets $350,000 should receive a greater score (as described in the following paragraph) than the one netting $150,000, even though they both meet the MUST objective of $100,000 profit. The difference in profit between these alternatives should be considered in making a choice. Yet it will be overlooked in making such a choice, unless the desire to exceed the MUST is included as one of the WANT objectives.

To judge the performance of each alternative against the WANT objectives, the manager should score each of them against each one of the objectives separately. He can use a numerical scoring scale for this, say 1 to 10, provided that the best alternative receives the top score. The other alternatives are then scored relative to this top score. Where there is no apparent difference between the performance of two alternatives, the same scores can be assigned. Or simple rank-ordering of alternatives can be substituted for a scoring scale with the highest number assigned to the best alternative. If there are three alternatives, the best might receive a score of 3, the next best 2, and so on. Here, too, tie scores can be used.

These scores or rankings reflect the way that each alternative performs against the specific objectives. They do *not* reflect the relative importance or emphasis the manager has placed on each of these objectives. Therefore, to get an overall judgment of the relative worths of each alternative, the manager must multiply the score of each alternative by the weight he has assigned to each objective. This weighted score expresses the performance of the alternative with due regard to the facts of performance and the importance of that performance. The weighted scores can now be added up to give totals for each of the alternatives. These total figures give the relative position of each of the alternatives on those items of performance considered in the specific objectives.

Using numbers in this way does not make the decision for the manager. At each step he has made his judgment based upon the facts available, his experience, and the experience of others. The numbers only record the judgments he had made. They have no magic; they contain no more than the careful thought the manager has put into them as to what would be important in getting the job done, and the performance of each alternative as he knows it. The numbers only make it possible for him to deal systematically with a great many judgments without losing track of what he is trying to get done, and what he is considering as relevant.

5. *Choose the best alternative as a tentative decision.*

The alternative that receives the highest weighted score on performance against the objectives is presumably the best course of action to take. However, this is only a tentative decision. On the basis of the evidence so far considered, it has checked out as the best of the alternatives available, providing the most results and returns for the least in resources committed. However, it will not be a perfect choice; it may only be the least worst of the alternatives selected. But it will represent the most favorable balance between good and bad as these have been defined by the objectives set down. Most likely, the highest-scoring alternative will be a compromise between several alternatives. Each of these may be able to do parts of the job better than other alternatives, but only one rates high in getting the *whole* job done.

Moreover, this tentative decision may not be the best choice when everything has been considered. Whenever a manager chooses a way of correcting or improving something, he is choosing the kind of new change he wants to insert into the system. And change, as we have found in dealing with problem analysis, causes problems. Any action taken will inevitably produce effects; otherwise the manager would not bother to make the decision in the first place, for he is trying to achieve planned beneficial effect. But since change is what produces problems, it is possible that some of the effects produced by a course of action may be worse than the initial problem. A manager must find these problems out ahead of time, if they exist, rather than later, when all he can do is to grit his teeth and bear it. He must, therefore, assess the consequences of his choice as completely as he can. This is good decision-making insurance.

6. *Assess the adverse consequences of the tentative decision.*

A manager should take the best alternatives and consider them independently, visualizing each as though it were already in operation. He should question the effect the alternative will have on other things, and the effect that other events will have on it. He is not reconsidering the attainment of objectives, but he is estimating the future possible effects of the action necessary to attain them. For example, if cost were an objective, he would not consider the cost of attaining each alternative as a consequence, but would weigh the possible effects and trends of these costs over a period of time. He should ask: "If we were to do this, then what would happen as a result? What could go wrong?" At this point, he is looking for trouble, trying to find the potential breakdowns and shortcomings that have escaped his notice so far. These will be hidden and obscure. They will lie primarily along the lines of contact between the proposed course of action and other activities going on in the company. Here are some promising places a manager might look for trouble:

People
    Motivation and attitudes
    Skills and abilities
    Performance and productivity
    Development and growth
    Health and safety
Organization
    Relationships among units, functions, persons
    Communications
    Responsibility and delegation
    Formal and informal organization
    Coordination
External Influences
    Economic trends
    Competition
    Company image
    Legal and government

Facilities and Equipment
  Space
  Flexibility and adaptability
  Location
  Compatibility
Ideas and Processes
  Security, proprietary position
  Adaptability
Material
  Sources and availability
  Quality
  Handling and storage
Money
  Capital or fixed
  Costs and expenses
  Return
Output
  Quality
  Quantity
  Pace and timing
Personal
  Goals and plans
  Family
  Strengths and weaknesses
  Interests

The manager can ask others on his staff to help him find holes in his proposed decision. A professional pessimist or "nit-picker" on the staff is a good man for this. A close examination of the decision may turn up some new objectives that the manager wants to crank back into the original set, to be weighted and treated like any other objective. He may also find some real dangers that apply to one course of action and no other. He may find a great deal that he wouldn't know about if he hadn't looked.

Not all consequences, however, will be equally threatening to the decision. Some will be more serious than others if they actually occur; some will be fatal to the plan of action while others will merely hurt it. The consequences should be weighted in terms of seriousness and impact, just as the WANT objectives were weighted in terms of importance. In addition to seriousness, the manager needs to know how *probable* any of these consequences are. He should estimate how likely any one of them is of happening and put this down beside each alternative. For example, he may know that coordination almost always breaks down, and so give this a 90 per cent probability. On the other hand, he may estimate that there is only a 10 per cent probability of a lost-time accident in the plant. If he considers these two consequences equal in seriousness in their impact on his decision, but obviously unequal in probability, he should recognize that the more probable consequence, the breakdown in coordination, poses the greatest threat to the completion of his project. But he is most concerned with the *total* degree of threat an alternative poses to the accomplishment of his objectives. To get an expression of this total threat, he can multiply the seriousness weight by the probability estimate. This will give him a measure of the size of the sword that hangs over his head if he chooses this or that course of action.

Careful evaluation of the consequences may show the manager that, because of the adverse consequences he has uncovered, he does not dare adopt what he thought was the best alternative. He may find that the alternative with second best performance of the WANTS is, on the whole, the better bet because it is safer and carries fewer threats.

If this is the case, he is in the position of having to balance performance on the objectives against the consequences. He cannot resolve this by adding and subtracting numbers. The numbers that indicate the threat of the consequences cannot be put into the decision analysis format, since objectives and consequences are apples and oranges. He can only judge the magnitude of each and use his best, most informed common sense as to how they balance out. He is betting present performance against the possibility of future problems. But at least he knows what he is judging. He has the luxury of worrying now, in place of salvaging a catastrophe at a later date. If he decides to discard his previous "best" course of action in favor of the second best, with a lower performance but also lower threat, he should check through the next poorest alternative just to be sure. He should continue this process until he has clearly found an alternative that provides him with a favorable balance of advantage and disadvantage.

7. *Control effects of the final decision by preventing adverse consequences and by follow-up.*

This final stage of decision making is critical to the whole procedure. If a manager, having become clear in his mind that he has chosen the best way to achieve his objective, simply gives the necessary orders and moves on to the next problem, he is automatically inviting a lot of serious trouble. Once he starts to implement his decision, every adverse consequence he considered earlier becomes a potential problem. Now, before it is too late, he has the opportunity of preventing these consequences from ever coming to pass. He can analyze them for possible causes and then take preventive actions to remove those causes.

Or, failing to remove a possible cause, he can decide on a contingency action to be taken if and when the potential problem actually occurs. As we have already indicated, these two kinds of action are part of the procedures of potential problem analysis which are described in the final chapter of this text.

Finally, before he puts his plan into effect he should recognize that other difficulties will occur if he does not carefully plan for implementing his decision. To help assure this implementation he should take the following five steps:

1. Set up controls and reporting procedures so that he can know the progress of his plan against the schedule worked out for putting it into effect.

2. Follow-up on his orders to know that they have been received and understood.

3. Determine responsibility for carrying out his orders, and verify that this is understood.

4. Set up specific reporting dates at which to measure the action being taken.

5. Set up a warning system that will tell him as early as possible if his plan is getting into trouble in any respect.

Before undertaking these last actions, the manager should be sure that he is well versed in the preceding phases of decision analysis that have been outlined in this chapter. To help make these clearer and more specific, let us consider the decision that has to be made by a manager who, though comfortably situated in a pleasant home, suddenly finds that a new superhighway is going to come right through his living room, and that he will have to buy himself a new house within sixty days. This constitutes a problem for him. He does not have to analyze it for cause, since this is known. When the city engineers knocked on his door, they informed him of the route and schedule of construction. He will receive a fair price for his present home, but he cannot appeal or influence the action taken by the highway department. So he moves directly into decision making.

He starts by considering his objectives. He works in a large city and there are thousands of houses on the market from which to choose, but he doesn't want just any house. He wants as nearly perfect a home for himself and his family as he can get, within what he can afford. If he is going to recognize this superlative domicile when he sees it he will have to begin by setting down his specifications in terms of what he wants it to be and to do for him. His set of objectives will form the yardstick against which he will measure the various houses he looks at.

The manager sits down and begins thinking about his objectives. First he thinks about the MUST objectives, what he has to have in his new house. He considers his resources, the money he has in the bank, and what he could afford to pay each month in taxes, insurance, principal, and interest. He thinks about his family and decides he must have four bedrooms and two baths; he thinks about the daily commuting trip to the office and decides he does not want to live in the city, but that he cannot be farther away than forty-five minutes' driving time from his downtown parking lot. The final MUST is that he has to have occupancy of the house within sixty days.

Then the manager turns to the WANT objectives, what he would like to achieve in buying this new house. He starts by looking at the MUST objectives he has already set out. Some of these he further qualifies as WANT objectives; for example, he had set an absolute limit of $10,000 on the down payment but he would like to spend less if he could arrange it, and therefore "minimum down payment" becomes one of his WANT objectives. He does the same with the monthly payment objective. Then he adds other WANT objectives that were indicated by his resources; for instance, he wants to be able to use his present furnishings and appliances and he wants a two-car garage. He wants public transportation nearby, with the shopping center and the schools close to home also. Eventually he ends up with a list of six MUST objectives and eighteen WANT objectives as illustrated in Figure 25.

Next the manager goes over these WANT objectives and establishes their relative weights, using the scale of 1 to 10, with the most important WANT receiving the number 10. As he gives each objective more thorough consideration, he changes his preliminary weights until he has achieved a set of numbers representing the relative importance that he places on each objective. He is careful to put into the process at this point the best thinking of his wife and others affected by the move. He emerges with "lowest monthly payment" as most important, and "workshop space" and "large, modern kitchen with a view" as least, with a weight of 2 each.

Having established and classified his objectives according to importance, the manager now sits down with a real estate agent and presents his list of MUSTS and WANTS. The agent has more than 1,000 houses listed in his files, but the manager's set of MUST objectives reduces the number of possibilities to a fraction of what the agent has on file. For example, he can eliminate from consideration all houses that require a down payment of more than

MUST OBJECTIVES: Resource limits and required results

Down payment not to exceed $10,000
Monthly payment (principal, interest, taxes, and insurance)
     not to exceed $300
Minimum of four bedrooms
Minimum of two bathrooms
Location outside of downtown area, within 45-minutes
     driving time to office parking lot
Occupancy within 60 days

WANT OBJECTIVES: Best use of resources, maximum results and returns,
                   minimum disadvantage

	Weight
Minimum down payment	6
Lowest monthly payment	10
Location conveniently close to work	7
Able to use present furnishings, drapes	5
Shelter for two cars	4
Public transportation nearby	4
Location convenient to elementary and high schools .	8
Location convenient to shopping center, stores	7
Workshop and storage space available	2
Stable resale value	7
Attractive; modern style and appearance	5
Good landscaping; trees, shrubs	4
Large play area for kids	5
Large, modern kitchen with a view	2
Large, comfortable family room	3
Location on quiet street, in good neighborhood	4
Minimum maintenance cost to house	7
Minimum risk - tax increase or special assessments .	4

FIGURE 25   A typical objective-setting worksheet containing MUSTS and
WANTS, with appropriate weights added, for the house-purchase example
described in the text.

$10,000 or a monthly payment of over $300; all two-
bedroom bungalows, three-bedroom small houses, old
houses with only one bath, houses in the downtown area;
houses more than forty-five minutes away from work, and
those requiring more than sixty days waiting before moving in. By setting out his MUST objectives the manager
has saved both himself and the real estate agent a lot of

time and money. He realizes that, in the same way, in his daily work he could save time for his subordinates and suppliers, by setting out clearly the objectives he wants to achieve.

The real estate agent, guided by the manager's objectives, comes up with three houses that passed the MUSTS and seemed to fit the WANT objectives most nearly. The manager then examines each one of the houses in turn, going down the list of objectives and comparing the characteristics of each house against each objective. He checks the MUST objectives first and finds that only two of the three houses qualify as possible alternatives, since alternative B requires a monthly payment of $370 which is above the $300 limit the manager had set. This one had slipped by in the first screening, and it is now marked NO/GO and eliminated from further consideration. Then the manager tests each of the two remaining houses point by point against the WANT objectives he has set out. Using a 1 to 10 scale, he scores each house against each of the eighteen WANT objectives, then multiplies each score by the corresponding weight he had originally assigned to each objective. This gives him a final weighted score for each house on each of these objectives. The total weighted scores for each house represent the performance of that alternative, with due regard to the importance of the objectives considered.

The results of the manager's calculations are shown on the decision analysis worksheet illustrated in Figure 26. It will be seen that the total weighted score of house A is 804 as opposed to 848 for house C. This made house C the best choice in the overall judgment of the manager. It might

DECISION ANALYSIS WORKSHEET

MUSTS:		Alternative A			Alternative B	Alternative C		
Down payment not over $10,000		$7,500 ✓			$9,500 ✓	$6,000 ✓		
Monthly payment not over $300		300 ✓			370 NO GO	280 ✓		
Minimum of four bedrooms		4				4		
Minimum of two bathrooms		2				2		
Location, outside downtown area, not more than 45-minutes driving time		30 minutes ✓				25 minutes ✓		
Occupancy within 60 days		45 days ✓				45 days ✓		

WANTS:	wt.	(A)	sc.	wt. sc.		(C)	sc.	wt. sc.
Minimum down payment	6	$7,500	9	54		$6,000	10	60
Lowest monthly payment, including taxes	10	300	9	90		280	10	100
Location convenient to work	7	good	10	70		OK	8	56
Use present furnishings, drapes	5	good	8	40		very good	10	50
Shelter for two cars	4	carport	7	28		garage	10	40
Public transportation nearby	4	bus	9	36		bus close	10	40
Location convenient to elementary and high schools	8	1/2 mile	7	56		1/4 mile	10	80
Location convenient to shopping center, stores, and facilities	7	1 mile	7	49		1/2 mile	10	70
Workshop and storage space available	2	large	10	20		poor	3	6
Stable resale value	7	good	10	70		good	10	70
Attractive; modern style and appearance	5	new	8	40		excellent	10	50
Good landscaping; trees, shrubs	4		10	40		OK	7	28
Large play area for kids	5	unfenced	7	35		fenced	10	50
Large, modern kitchen with view	2	good	10	20		good	10	20
Large, comfortable family room	3	yes	10	30		none	0	0
Location on quiet street, in good neighborhood	4	good	10	40		fair	8	32
Minimum maintenance cost to house	7	good	10	70		average	8	56
Minimum risk-tax increase or special assessments	4	high	4	16		low	10	40
PERFORMANCE TOTAL, WANT OBJECTIVES				804				848

FIGURE 26 A typical decision analysis worksheet containing relevant facts, weights, scores, and weighted scores for the house-purchase example described in the text.

not, of course, be the best choice for another manager, whose judgment and experience might have produced a somewhat different series of WANT objectives and relative weightings. But for this manager the calculations shown here gave him a clear view of what he had considered, how he had arrived at this preliminary decision, and where he should now look for any adverse consequences.

Now the manager begins looking for any adverse consequences that might come from his tentative decision to buy house C. He thinks about potential breakdowns and shortcomings in the house that might have escaped him in his first exploration. He goes back to look over both house A and house C again, and he finds several possible consequences that disturb him. He notices marks in the basement of house C that might indicate a flooding condition during heavy rainfall. Also he realizes that the new construction just starting on the addition to the shopping center will probably mean heavier traffic in front of house C, which is on a street connecting two main routes to the center. Then he starts thinking about the country club's location on the other side of town; he would be using it a lot, he knows, for business contacts, and the prospect of round trips through town to get there and back doesn't please him. And as he looks at the back yard of house C, he knows it wouldn't be big enough to satisfy his wife, who is a gardening enthusiast.

Now he considers the possible adverse consequences of buying house A, and he finds out that one of the men working for him owns the house across the street. That could mean awkward social relationships for him, since he does not believe in socializing with subordinates, and this man is rather aggressively social. Then he also recalls that his wife has told him she has discovered that in that neighborhood there are very few children of the same age as their children, and he knows this could mean unhappiness at home.

He puts all these possible adverse consequences down on a sheet, and scores each one according to his estimate of the probability of its happening and its seriousness if it did happen. He multiplies these two scores for each consequence, then adds them up, and he discovers that on balance house A, which gave him less of what he wanted, does not carry the heavy threat of consequences that house C does. A worksheet showing his calculations appears in Figure 27.

The manager, therefore, subsequently bought house A, and later he was happy in his choice. That next winter was one of the wettest on record, and the man who bought house C had, among other things, 9 inches of water in the basement.

Note that in choosing house A the manager knew why and on what grounds he was doing so. He did not take the "cancel-out" approach used by some managers in decision making. In this approach, the assumption is that an advantage cancels out a disadvantage so that things even up. This is not so. If there is a disadvantage attached to an alternative, finding an advantage does not get rid of it. Once the decision is made, the disadvantage will have to be lived with until it is removed by corrective action of some sort. The only safe way to deal with disadvantages in decision making is to recognize them and to keep them visible before one throughout the process. A final decision or course of action can then be made in full knowledge of

POSSIBLE ADVERSE CONSEQUENCES WORKSHEET

Alternate A	Prob-ability	Serious-ness	P x S	Alternate C	Prob-ability	Serious-ness	P x S
Awkward social relationship – subordinate lives across the street	8	4	32	Risk of basement flooding – major repairs	9	9	81
Few playmates for children in neighborhood	7	7	49	Heavier traffic due to addition to new shopping center	5	9	45
				Inconvenience of country club across town	9	9	81
				Poor land for wife's gardening	9	10	90
			81				297

FIGURE 27 A typical adverse consequences worksheet containing the possible consequences, scored according to probability and seriousness, for the two alternatives in the house-purchase example described in the text.

the disadvantages rather than by glossing over defects and hiding them. Having all the assessments that enter into a decision visibly set forth is a major advantage in itself. For one may readily go back to reexamine the judgments made and consider corrective actions that can be taken to improve an already good alternative.

Some managers may question whether it is necessary to go through these stages of decision making so carefully and specifically. To be sure, many of the decisions a manager faces in day-to-day operation involve fairly simple choices and relatively small amounts of information. He can set objectives, assign weights of importance, consider and assess alternatives, and do this all in his head rather rapidly. If the decision process remains simple, he won't need a complicated matrix or format to arrive at his conclusions. This is the way it ought to be. But any time a manager feels that he runs a chance of confusion, or of losing a judgment along the line, or of missing something, he should take a fail-safe approach and doodle his thoughts down on paper. He can always go back and correct or improve something he has put on paper; but he can't do this if he tries to keep all the relevant information in his head.

A systematic recording of information on problems and decisions is especially useful in meetings. Whenever a group of managers confers on such matters, two things become very important: the retrieval of information and the combination of judgments. In reaching a decision, managers need not only to store information but to have easy access to it, and they also need to pool their judgments on alternative actions. These needs can be readily met with the system of decision analysis we have described.

It is clear that every decision that is made will be a compromise in one way or another, balancing advantages against disadvantages, trading this objective off against that one, accepting partial performances where complete performance is not possible. The manager has to arrive at the best compromise he can, the one that gives him the most in results for the least cost. To do this he has to make the best use of the information he possibly can, and that calls for a set of disciplined orderly procedures for working through and holding the data available to him. The methods outlined in this chapter will not guarantee successful decision making simply because so much of what is involved in decision making is uncertain and deals with future probabilities. It is all the more critical, therefore, that the manager does everything he can to assure that he is getting the most use of the information he does have. In this way he is most likely to be right more times than wrong. If he can reduce that uncertainty by only a little bit, through following a systematic approach, he may have gained a great deal.

As we have already indicated, one of the most effective ways to assure the success of a major decision is to foresee and forestall those adverse consequences that such a decision often produces. A manager can do this by analyzing such problems before they develop. In fact, a systematic analysis of potential problems is the best means, not only of making past decisions succeed, but of making future decisions fewer and easier. We shall devote the following final chapter to the procedures of potential problem analysis.

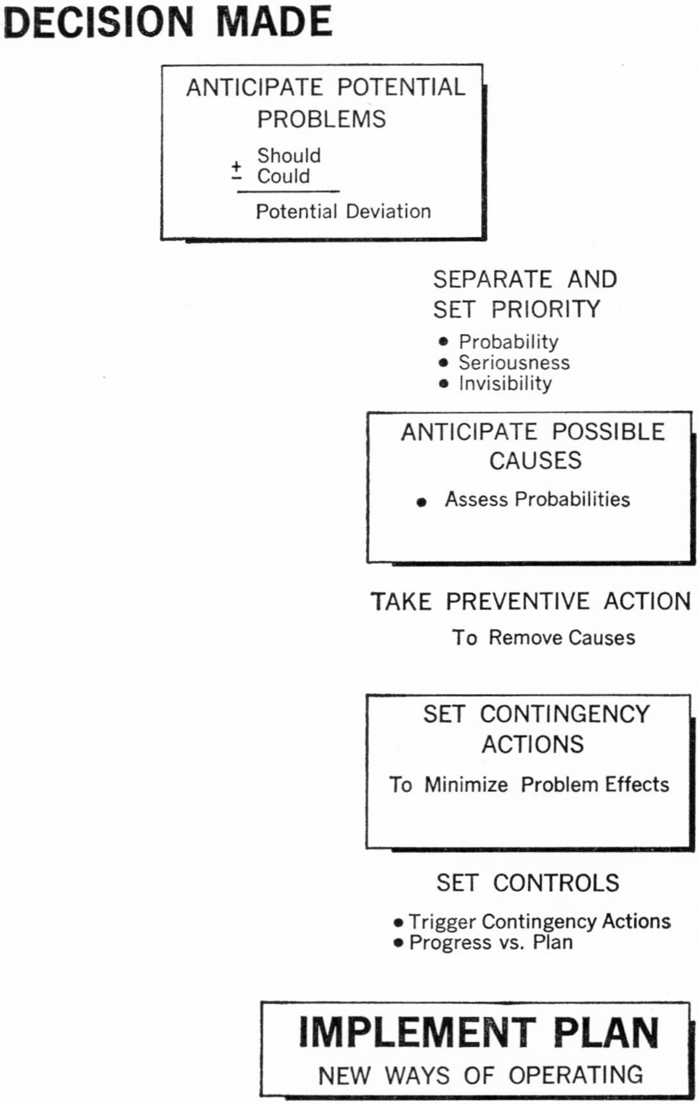

DECISION MADE

ANTICIPATE POTENTIAL
PROBLEMS

$\pm$ Should
Could

Potential Deviation

SEPARATE AND
SET PRIORITY

• Probability
• Seriousness
• Invisibility

ANTICIPATE POSSIBLE
CAUSES

• Assess Probabilities

TAKE PREVENTIVE ACTION

To Remove Causes

SET CONTINGENCY
ACTIONS

To Minimize Problem Effects

SET CONTROLS

• Trigger Contingency Actions
• Progress vs. Plan

IMPLEMENT PLAN
NEW WAYS OF OPERATING

FIGURE 28   The process of potential problem analysis solves problems in advance either by removing their causes so they cannot happen, or by minimizing their effects if they do happen. Efficient direction and control clearly depend upon good potential problem analysis that sets the basis for preventive and contingency actions.

CHAPTER **11**

Potential Problem Analysis

By far the most rewarding actions any manager might take are those that can be taken *before* any particular problem developed. This kind of action involves the technique of analyzing potential problems. The aim of such analysis is to find feasible, economic actions that can be taken against the possible causes of problems that have not yet happened, as a means of avoiding trouble. This gives the manager a chance to get ahead of the game in either of two ways: he can either act to prevent possible problems from coming to pass, or he can act to minimize the effects that these possible problems will produce if they do occur.

The systematic analysis of potential problems is still rare. Yet it is not difficult to show that skill in analyzing and preventing or minimizing potential problems can provide the most returns for the effort and time expended by a manager. The point is so well-known that it has become an axiom: an ounce of prevention is worth a pound of cure. So few managers apply the axiom, however, that it is reasonable to assume there are major obstacles preventing them from doing so. One obstacle is that managers are generally far more concerned with correcting today's problems than with preventing or minimizing tomorrow's. This is not surprising, of course, since the major rewards in money and promotion so often go to those who show the best records of solving current problems in management, and there is rarely a direct reward for those whose foresight keeps problems from occurring.

There are also other reasons why so few managers analyze and deal with potential problems. There is the common tendency to overlook the critical consequences of an action. Such consequences may be missed because they seem too disagreeable or unpalatable to face, or the consequence may be literally invisible. Let us first consider an example of the unfaced consequence. A manager and his wife one night invented a children's game based on one they had heard their children call "I.C.U.C." (for "I see you see"). Delighted by this invention, the manager mentioned it later to his friends in his office, who not only showed enthusiasm for the game, but they and their wives offered to help the manager and his wife develop it for the market. Together this group of husbands and wives worked on perfecting models, checked production costs, and tested the game out on other children in four different states. Their enthusiasm kept rising, and a corporation was organized with $6,000 in capital supplied by six of the men. They decided to make 10,000 of the games, and, with everyone pitching in, the first 1,000 were finally finished and mailed to drugstores, gas stations, and other outlets they had decided upon as the best markets. Then they waited expectantly for the first returns. But not one single inquiry was received, not a game was sold. Stunned, they sent out tracers and discovered the fact they had failed to face: the game simply did not appeal to anyone in the markets they had picked. It was a dud. But not one of the managers who invested in the venture had stopped to ask, "What if it fails?" Had they asked this question, they might have been ready with an alternate marketing action, such as checking with a big mail-order house to see if the game might be sold through its distribution channels. Instead, all the investors simply took their losses and gave up.

In another case, an invisible consequence nearly ruined a plan for attracting more young people in the community to become employees of an aluminum-fabricating plant. The company had decided to offer a guided tour of the plant to local boys and girls in the hope that this might increase its share of this manpower market. Great care was taken to see that no physical hazards were overlooked; cutting edges on machinery were checked for shielding, drivers of fork-lift trucks were cautioned in advance, and other similar safety steps were taken. When the young people came through the plant all went well until one foreman, who was talking to a small group, noticed a boy lift his foot up and look at his shoe: the whole sole was missing. The foreman instantly realized what happened: the boy had put his foot on an ingot of aluminum, not realizing it was hot enough to burn his foot to a crisp. The boy couldn't see any danger because there is no difference in appearance between an aluminum ingot at room temperature and one at 1200 degrees F. Fortunately the boy wasn't hurt, and the foreman just managed to prevent another boy from sitting down on a pile of hot ingots. But note that this hazard had remained invisible, not only to the touring group, but to those who had really tried to foresee the possible risks of such a tour. People who work with aluminum are accustomed to wetting the tips of their fingers, then testing ingots, much as grandma used to test a hot iron in the days before thermostats. The practice is so commonplace in the industry that the danger of hot ingots remained completely hidden from the safety engineer who had checked for hazards before the tour.

Now consider another obstacle to the analysis and prevention of potential problems. This is the common conviction of managers and others who make plans that any plan of theirs is eminently workable, or they wouldn't have suggested it in the first place. They find it very difficult to ask the question, "What could go wrong?" It is hard for them to get accustomed to the idea of looking for potential problems. What could go wrong is often beyond their experience as planners and therefore seems outlandish to them. They see little use in looking for trouble. Yet the evidence is all to the contrary. All the examples of problem handling we have seen or heard of have shown us that things *have* gone wrong, *continue* to go wrong, and, one can believe, *always will* go wrong. Looking for possible problems and what their effects might be is therefore an inevitable function of intelligent management.

The need to analyze potential problems shows up everywhere. For example, take one of the recent attempts to help feed an underdeveloped African nation. It was decided that some of the frozen chickens the United States government had stockpiled could be sent over, provided the fowl were unfrozen and canned, since refrigeration was not yet available in that African country. Some canning companies showed this could be readily done, and contracts were awarded for the work. Thousands of cases were soon shipped. Then the potential problems became problems with a vengeance: the cans of chicken swelled and exploded in the hot sun, showering putrid meat over the African landscape. The cause was eventually found: no one had foreseen the difference between the methods used in canning and handling a few cans during their preliminary testing procedures, and the canning and handling of thousands of cases of cans. On a mass-production basis, some chickens were canned before being completely thawed out, and the steaming process was deficient because too many were stacked in the ovens. The result was high bacteria counts and putrid chicken.

But this was only the first problem to emerge. Other more serious ones began to appear. The African people were, of course, offended, and then Communist propaganda charged that the American people, who had excellent refrigeration equipment and would not themselves stand for spoiled food, nevertheless thought that all black people and others outside the United States didn't know the difference between good and bad food. The effects of these problems may last for years. Yet, like most problems, they might have been foreseen and prevented had those involved asked, "What could go wrong?" and then taken steps to prevent any of the possible fiascos.

Still another obstacle to the analysis of potential problems is the tendency of people to think, on the basis of a superficial examination, that they fully understand all of its implications. They may feel themselves to be in agreement on the intent of a plan, for example, and see no reason to probe further into it. Then, when the plan goes into operation, they see for the first time that it will produce effects they did not specifically agree to. But by then the opportunity for prevention has passed, and a problem to be solved has arrived. The further an action under a plan is removed from the parties in time or in distance or in culture, the easier it will be for any of them to see the operation of the plan in a different light from that which they had in mind when they entered into the plan in the first place. This kind of potential problem remains invisible until some specific case arises that gives the problem its form and content.

A potential invisible problem of this kind developed not long ago in an auto plant where both management and labor had adopted an unusual profit-sharing plan. The plan was hailed by both sides, and its gist was that the employees would share in the benefits of any increased productivity, with each employee's contributions to savings being credited as shares in a central fund. The plan worked fine for some time; productivity did increase and a lot of savings were realized. However, one potential problem, unrecognized by either management or labor, began to develop: one worker, who had earnestly tried to increase his production and cut costs, suddenly needed money for a family emergency and asked the company for his share of the accumulated savings fund. But management refused his request, citing the provisions of the plan that stipulated no withdrawals could be made for a certain period of years after the savings of each year were credited to the employee. The plan made no provision for withdrawal of funds in case of emergencies. Management held that it could not grant this man's request since this would establish a precedent that could start a flood of requests for withdrawals and thus upset the whole financial basis of the plan. The union argued there was no reason why a few shares of the savings fund couldn't be released for the emergency needs of an employee. So, the plan produced bitterness because no one thought in the beginning to ask the question, "How will the plan be seen later by the participants when they need money and can't get it?" Had that been asked, the potential problems raised by emergency personal needs would undoubtedly have become visible.

Where potential problems involve both the company and the individual employee, there are always likely to be complications, and in analyzing such problems a manager has to distinguish between company and personal objectives. For example, a manager was recounting to a group of managers how he overlooked the possible consequences of appointing a new regional supervisor. When his boss, who had been studying potential problem analysis, asked him if he had considered how the appointment might affect the supervisor personally, the manager said he suddenly saw the point. "It was like turning on a faucet I'd never turned on before. All of a sudden all the information we had about this fellow started coming out, and we realized that the appointment would require him to move, to take his kids out of high school, and make a lot of other changes that could upset him. So we decided to rethink our decision." But at this point in his story the other managers broke in with strong objections. They didn't think the manager should decide for or against a candidate for a new job on the basis of what the consequences might be to the candidate personally. They insisted that a good manager wants to look out for himself, as an individual, and wouldn't want his superiors dropping him as a candidate for promotion simply because they thought he might not like the personal hardships that would result. Such consequences, in their opinion, were the manager's private responsibility; the company should concern itself only with those consequences that would affect the company and its objectives.

From the foregoing examples it is clear that the analysis of potential problems can be extremely useful. Such analysis, however, requires a different approach to causes from that used in problem analysis. In problem analysis the cause has happened, and the manager is looking for only one cause in order to know what corrective action to take. But in potential problem analysis both the deviations and the causes are possibilities only, and the manager must decide which actions are going to keep these possible causes from occurring. Any one of these potential problems, produced by any possible cause, might wreck or jeopardize the action a manager has decided to take. Therefore he has to consider them all, and he has to have some orderly way of doing this. He can do this if he systematically asks and gets the answers to seven questions. These seven questions should be considered consecutively as follows:

1. *What could go wrong?* The importance of this question has already been indicated. The plan of action a manager works out is really a series of "shoulds"; performance points at which certain things are supposed to hap-

pen. So the manager must go over his plan and think of the problems that might crop up. He can find plenty of these potential problems if he looks carefully at those elements where trouble so often starts. Here are six sources of potential problems:

- Where something new, complex, or unfamiliar is tried
- When deadlines are tight
- When a sequence is critical or has impact on others
- When an alternative is missing
- When things involve more than one person, function, or department
- Where responsibility is hard to assign, or is outside the manager's area

Perhaps none of the potential problems a manager foresees will appear. But a smart manager believes in Murphy's Law: "If it can go wrong, it will." So he lists all potential problems, and he will probably end up with a score or more.

2. *What, specifically, is each problem?* An accurate description of each potential problem is needed to tell the manager what it is, where it will occur, when, and in what degree. He need not be concerned with the IS NOT of each problem, since he is not trying to find the cause of a problem already in existence.

3. *How risky is each problem?* A manager cannot expect to cope with every one of the potential problems he finds; he has to cull out the small risks and concentrate on those that are more threatening to his plan. So he sets priority on potential problems according to two criteria:

1. How serious will it be if it happens?
2. How probable is it that it might happen?

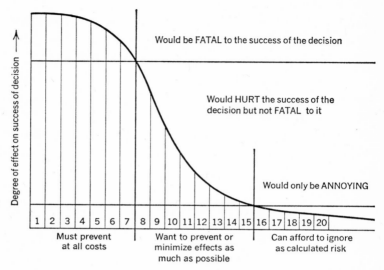

Potential Problems which might have an effect on the success of a decision

FIGURE 29   This chart shows the declining degree of threat that three classes of potential problems hold for the success of a decision. Reading from left to right, some potential problems would kill the decision, others would cripple it, and still others would only shake it a little. The great failures in managerial decision making have almost all come about because the managers involved did not recognize, or ignored, a "fatal" potential problem.

He combines the two judgments he makes in answering these questions to determine the total risk of a potential problem. Those possible problems he considers to be the greatest risks, i.e., those that are very serious and very likely to happen, can be fatal to his plan, and he *must* do something about them. Those possible problems he finds less serious and less likely can be painful, and he will *want* to do something about these. The rest of the potential problems that entail small risk will be merely annoying, and he can ignore them as calculated and accepted risks. A graph of the risks inherent in twenty potential problems anticipated in a hypothetical plan or decision might look like the one shown in Figure 29.

4. *What are the possible causes of each problem?* A manager cannot analyze for causes as he did in problem analysis, because the causes have not happened. But he can list all the possible causes he sees in a given problem, drawing heavily upon his judgment and experience. Many of these possible causes will never come into being to produce a problem, but he has no way of knowing this since he is dealing with possibilities only.

5. *How probable is each possible cause?* Here again the manager relies on his judgment and experience to assess the probability that a particular cause will occur. He will usually find many different possible causes for each possible problem, and he can then rate each of these causes as to its probability. For example, one potential high-risk problem might be a costly delay in delivery of essential equipment, and among the possible causes a manager might find these: bad weather, a railroad or teamsters strike, local traffic, clerical errors, poor coordination, machine breakdown, shortage of personnel, fire in supplier's plant, accident in carting, national holiday, etc. By going over each possible cause and estimating how likely it is to occur if no action is taken, the manager discovers which causes he should give the most attention to.

6. *How can a possible cause be prevented, or its effects be minimized?* The best action a manager can take is preventive action that removes the possible cause completely,

or attempts to reduce the probability that the cause will occur. Since each potential problem may have many possible causes, he may need to apply several actions to prevent these causes. Each possible cause he prevents will reduce the probability that the problem itself will occur. After preventive action is taken, each cause also has a residual probability; this probability is the likelihood of its happening after his best efforts to prevent it have failed.

In potential problem analysis, as in problem analysis, the manager has to use the stair-step process described in Chapter 4. Unless he does this, he may not be able to think of a preventive action when he looks at a potential problem. For example, the potential problem may show up as a future inability to produce enough to meet expected demands. One possible cause of this might be a manpower shortage, and the manager has therefore to ask what action he can take to prevent such a shortage. He cannot tell what preventive action he might use until he examines the possible causes for the shortage, such as bad weather, a strike, a local holiday, etc. He then may have to consider these possible causes as problems, and to explore them in turn for possible causes, continuing this process to the point where he can take a simple preventive action.

Preventive actions will differ, of course, according to the seriousness or complications of the cause to be prevented. A fairly typical example of preventive action occurred when a manager in a large auto company began checking over his plans for getting a special model from Detroit to Europe. He went over the details of his shipping plan that called for rail shipment in a special car to New York harbor, transshipment to the *Queen Mary*'s dock in the North River, and another transshipment to a rail car on the continent. Everything looked fine, except that no one had made any arrangements to get the model from the rail car in New York to the *Queen Mary*'s dock. The manager immediately canceled his original plan to fly to Europe and instead flew to New York. There he made arrangements to have the model transferred to the *Queen Mary*'s dock on a split-second schedule, since there was barely enough time to accomplish this before the ship sailed. Having prevented a serious potential problem from occurring by eliminating its possible cause, he then flew to Europe to make sure everything there went off as planned.

In another case, a serious potential problem was prevented only by a major corporate decision involving a twenty-year commitment. An international mining company decided to open up an extremely rich property it owned in Canada. The area was largely undeveloped, roads were poor, and the nearest town of 1,600 people had no modern urban conveniences, not even a sewage system. The company planned to employ some 3,500 in this project, and when the managers from the company asked if schools could be provided for the new employees' families, the local governing board saw that this overnight demand for schools was far beyond anything the modest community could expect to provide. But once this potential problem and its cause were identified, the company and the community agreed on preventive action: the company would pay its taxes to the community for twenty years in advance, thereby giving the local board funds to build new schools. The company got a bargain in taxes by paying them all at once at one rate, avoiding any possible future tax rises; and the community got a bargain in financial assistance for schooling that would make possible a project which would greatly benefit the town. Both parties benefited from the good community relations that resulted from the company's preventive action.

Still another example illustrates that a preventive action may involve simply a change in approach to a potential problem. In this case, a large food manufacturer had acquired three plants of a small baking company and was pressing to bring their operating costs in line with the parent company's standards. Two of the small plants gave no trouble, but costs in the third plant, which had been run somewhat paternalistically, remained too high despite stern efforts to discipline its employees. The manager in the parent company who was responsible for this cost program had about decided to install an industrial engineer at the high-cost plant, who would set up production quotas and generally tighten up the operation. But before this plan was carried out, the manager talked it over with a group of managers who were studying the concepts and procedures described in this text. The other managers promptly came up with a lot of potential problems; they pointed out that the industrial engineer and his methods would be a real threat to the manager of the high-cost plant, who was generally considered very competent in operating techniques, as well as a threat to other personnel at that location. They suggested that the plant manager be approached quite differently by means of three preventive actions: (1) talking with him to emphasize that the

parent company wasn't being critical of his work but trying to bring all its plants up to comparable standards;
(2) explore with him what was different about his plant
that made costs high and let him work out his own problems; (3) tolerate the plant's excessive costs for a couple
of months until all employees understood why stopwatch
studies were going to be necessary on particular jobs.
These three actions made no change in the company's objectives but anticipated what could go wrong in a sticky
situation.

7. *How can the most serious potential problems be handled?* Whenever a manager thinks a potential problem is
so serious he cannot rely on preventive actions to remove
the cause or reduce its probability significantly, he should
prepare contingency actions to be adopted immediately if
the problem occurs. If a cheap preventive action is possible, he will apply this first in the hope that it will make the
contingency action unnecessary. But if the contingency action does become necessary, he should be ready with action
complete enough to offset or minimize the effects he thinks
the potential problem could produce. This kind of
standby, fail-safe action corresponds to the lifeboats on an
"unsinkable" ship.

Contingency actions are called for where the stakes are
very high and where there is great risk that a failure at one
point in a plan will let the whole operation go down the
drain. A marketing manager in the headquarters of a large
equipment manufacturer found this out one Friday afternoon when he checked over an important promotion pro-

gram involving three different sales districts between Philadelphia and Washington. Although many had worked on the plan, which was to go into effect the following Monday, he discovered that the headquarters staff, the ad agency, and each district manager and dealer knew only part of the plan. The whole story was known only to the Eastern regional manager in Philadelphia who was coordinating things. The marketing manager realized at once that if this regional manager got sick, there would be chaos when the plan went into operation on Monday morning. So the marketing manager took a contingency action: he phoned the Philadelphia manager and asked him to brief one assistant on the whole plan, just in case. It was a rewarding move, for that afternoon the Philadelphia manager had a heart attack, and the whole program would have become chaotic if that one assistant had not been briefed in advance.

In another case, the director of a government agency had arranged for a prominent Senator to give the main address at the dedication ceremonies of a $10 million research center. After studying potential problem analysis, the director decided to examine this situation for possible problems. The most serious one was the possibility that the Senator might not be able to attend. So the director set up a plan for contingency action: he secured an appropriate substitute speaker and got an assistant to arrange for reprinting the programs in the event that the Senator canceled his speech. The night before the dedication ceremonies, the director got a call informing him that the Senator was ill and was entering a hospital. The director immediately called his substitute speaker, had his assistant carry out the plan for reprinting the programs, and notified others connected with the program. The revised ceremonies went off without a single hitch.

It should be noted, however, that there is a tendency for managers to proceed immediately with contingency actions and to ignore preventive actions. This is a mistake, for preventive actions are usually the least expensive, and preventing a problem is obviously better than having to take contingency actions. The manager's choice should be the action that gives the most results for the least cost and effort—which is what we mean by "efficient action."

For contingency actions, he must establish early warning mileposts in his plan that will alert him and tell him he *now* has a problem, and that any action from this point on will be coping with the effects of this problem. Such information mileposts can be set up so as to "trigger" the contingency action he has planned. This will tell him what information is needed, where the problem actually originated, where it will go, and who is responsible for applying the specific parts of the contingency action.

It is useful to arrange the elements of a potential problem in some chart form. A simple version of such a chart might look like the one shown on the next page.

However, the full analysis of a major potential problem requires much more detail and supporting information than goes into a simple chart. To show how complete and rewarding a full analysis can be, let us take the case of one manager who faced a tough weekend assignment. He had to arrange the move of his company's office furnishings

Potential Problem: LOSS OF MARKET FOR PRODUCT A			
Possible causes	Proba-bility	Actions	
		Preventive	Contingency
1. Competition	50%	a. Improve style b. Lower price c. Sell harder	a. Drop product
2. Public taste .changing	20%	a. More adver- tising b. Change style	a. Substitute new product

from the third floor of one building to the fourth floor of a
new building across the street in a downtown location. He
had to do this on Sunday, starting at 9 A.M., and he had to
have the job done by 3 P.M., when the president of the
corporation was going to lead an inspection party through
the new quarters. The manager was given to understand
that all depended upon him, and that the president would
be most unhappy if the move didn't go off smoothly and
on schedule.

The manager's first step was to work through a plan for
the move and schedule it, with all the work to be done by a
commercial mover using handtrucks because of the short
hauling distance involved. Then he systematically carried
out a potential problem analysis of his plan. He put down
the WHAT, WHERE, WHEN, and EXTENT of the project, and then thought through what could go wrong,
finding four major problems. Then he listed all the possible causes he could think of under each potential problem,
and assigned a probability percentage to each of nineteen
possible causes. Then he decided on preventive actions
that could be applied to each possible cause; and he

assigned a residual probability he thought each cause might have after the preventive actions had been taken. Then he put down contingency actions he could use to backstop each of the preventive actions. The tabulation he had when he finished his analysis is shown below:

ANALYSIS OF POTENTIAL PROBLEMS

What: The movement of furniture and office equipment is liable to get all fouled up.

Where: From third floor building A to fourth floor of new building B across street.

When: Sunday, starting 9 AM and finishing 3 PM for inspection.

Extent: Twenty desks and tables, forty file cabinets, typewriters, chairs, etc.

Possible causes	Proba-bility	Preventive actions	Resid-ual proba-bility	Contingent actions
A. *Move will take too long:*				
1. Stuff not packed, ready	70	Instruct; set deadline; inspect mid-PM Friday	5.	Have two-man packing crew on hand
2. Not enough movers show up	20	Check; get written commitment from movers	10	Know of backup commercial mover
3. Freight elevator not manned or operating	50	Check; arrange for operator	5	Have backup operator on call
4. Hand trucks not available	20	Check and arrange	0	Know where to borrow
5. Union or hours dispute arises	10	Check arrangements with mover	3	Clarify authority to bargain on spot
6. Lunch counters nearby are closed, no food	70	Check hours; locate nearest one that will be open	10	Know catering truck service to call
7. Abnormally heavy traffic on street in front	15	Check Sunday flow; obtain police rerouting	5	Have policeman on hand
8. Doors locked, no one has key	50	Get passkey	0	

ANALYSIS OF POTENTIAL PROBLEMS (Continued)

Possible causes	Proba-bility	Preventive actions	Resid-ual proba-bility	Contingent actions
B. Stuff will be mixed up, things all confused:				
1. Stuff not properly labeled	80	Instruct; inspect mid-PM Friday	10	Have assistant, who can label stuff
2. Destination areas not marked	90	Check; work out system of marking; signs put up	5	Have assistant who knows areas
3. Movers don't know where to put stuff	100	Layout rooms with chalk, use signs and labels	5	Have assistant who knows layout
4. Directions wrong, movers get confused	50	Preliminary briefing, appoint traffic captain	10	Be alert for signs of confusion
5. Someone else moving in, same time	10	Check with building superintendent	5	Rearrange schedule, set up aisles to keep separate
C. Stuff will be damaged:				
1. Breakables not properly packed	40	Instruct; provide packing materials, inspect	10	Have two-man packing crew on hand
2. Doors, corners, elevators not padded	100	Check for critical spots, arrange for padding	10	Have extra pads on hand
3. Boxes not used for typewriters, etc.	80	Instruct; provide boxes, inspect	5	Have extra boxes on hand
D. Stuff will be stolen, lost:				
1. Unauthorized people come in, take things	50	Place uniformed guards at doors; have mover post bond	5	Spotcheck against list
2. Desks, files not locked	40	Instruct, check locks	10	Have man lock same
3. No one policing, lax atmosphere	80	Have uniformed guard roving buildings; post warnings that place is under guard	5	Be on the alert for signs of lax atmosphere, theft

In the last week before the office move took place, the manager began to take his preventive actions, and then he saw the value of having analyzed for potential problems. Of the nineteen possible causes he had listed, eight would have occurred. He took care of each in turn:

- When he checked on packing, he found several people were going to be out of the office, and he arranged for others to pack their effects.
- When he checked on the freight elevator in the new building he found it was scheduled to be down for adjustment over the weekend of the move, and he arranged for the adjustment to be postponed.
- When he checked on lunch counters, he found that no one had thought of having lunch and that no food was available within four blocks, so he arranged for a catering truck to be on hand.
- When he checked on traffic, he found that fairly heavy churchbound traffic passed the buildings between 10:30 A.M. and noon. He obtained a police reroute for the critical Sunday.
- When he checked on destination areas, he found that no one had provided for marking them. He got someone to lay out the areas in chalk and to put up signs.
- When he asked, he found that someone else was moving on the same day, and he arranged for them to use the alley entrance.
- When he checked the route to be followed, he found three sharp corners that handtrucks would have trouble getting around, and he had the corners padded.
- His uniformed door guards apprehended and removed five unauthorized persons from the building. He later found that other companies had lost equipment to such "free help" on similar moves.

As a result of his foresight, the move went off smoothly. He was firmly convinced things would have been a shambles if he had not systematically analyzed the potential problems, and if he had not kept asking the questions that would reveal possible causes and suggest the actions he could take to prevent things from going wrong. He had learned that he could avoid or minimize the risks that any plan of his would inevitably face.

Basically, the systematic analysis of potential problems is the process of applying systematic forethought to the achievement of objectives. Without such forethought, managers are confined to the processes of systematic afterthought, which is what the analysis of existing problems involves. While extremely valuable, this is always one step behind the march of events. But a manager who has developed the capacities needed for the recognition of consequences and the analysis of potential problems, has moved into the select ranks of those who are competent to make and implement policy decisions about future operations. He has, in short, attained full stature as a rational manager.

APPENDIX

Notes on the Training Courses of Kepner-Tregoe and Associates, Inc., Princeton, New Jersey

The concepts and procedures described in this book have been developed by the authors and their associates through years of practical experience in training executives, managers, and supervisors. Training programs have been developed for senior and middle managers and for company officers (the APEX Course); for middle and junior managers and supervisors (the GENCO Course); for sales managers and supervisors (the VERTEX Course); and for managers in government agencies and other nonprofit organizations (the FBA Course). A course in trouble shooting and technical problem analysis is in the final stages of development. We have also trained and licensed managers as course leaders to conduct Kepner-Tregoe training inside their own companies, and have monitored their work in order to maintain the standards we have set. What follows is an explanation of why these courses were developed and how they are conducted.

Experience still seems to be the best teacher of problem-analyzing and decision-making skills. But on-the-job experience is too slow; it cannot meet the demands of the vast number of skilled managers needed in industry today. Moreover, managers do not naturally learn to solve problems well simply as a result of experience. Unlike scientists, doctors, engineers, lawyers, and other trained professionals, managers are left to learn by trial and error, and all too often they have no idea of what, why or where, or how they go wrong in solving their problems.

The basic reason for their difficulties is that the processes of problem analysis and decision making are *invisible*. The processes take place in the mind of a person, and it is not open to the scrutiny of others. No one can help, no one can point out oversights or errors or the inclusion of faulty assumptions. When the problem has been analyzed and the decision made, no one can be sure that there are no great flaws in the reasoning, and therefore in the conclusions as well. What is even more serious is that managers generally have no way of reviewing how they solve their problems, and so cannot benefit from their mistakes. They are usually too busy trying to find answers to the next problem waiting to be solved; they cannot step back mentally and examine the processes by which they thought their way through a problem and reached the decision. The higher the level in management, the more intangible the matters to be handled and the more difficult it is for the manager to know how well he is performing.

Thus, the primary purpose of the Kepner-Tregoe training courses is to show managers, in a short time, how to make the processes of problem analysis and decision making visible to themselves. Until these processes become visible to a manager, he cannot expect to improve them in himself. But once he is aware of what he does as he thinks his way through a problem, improvement is definitely possible. Research and experience have both shown that the skills of problem analysis and decision making depend more on what a man *does* with information than on his innate abilities. Finally, it should be emphasized that the manager who is skilled in problem analysis and decision making can improve these capacities in his subordinates and in others in his company.

What, then, makes a manager learn most rapidly? In any learning situation, three things must be present:

1. New ideas and skills or new ways of approaching old ideas and skills

2. An opportunity to put these innovations into practice

3. Feedback on (a) the results of the actions taken, and (b) the relation between what was done at each step and the end result

In short, the manager needs awareness of new concepts, practice in applying them, and feedback on the results of his performance. The kind of feedback is critical, for it will determine the kind of learning that takes place. It is not enough to know that the end results were poor. The feedback must also enable the learner to see *how* the ideas, specific procedures, and actions he used contributed to the final outcome. One learns by taking an idea, trying it out, and seeing how and why it works, or fails to work.

Management development courses generally do not provide such feedback. They present ideas but do not give the participant a chance to try these out. A manager usually must go back to his job with the ideas he has learned and hope for an opportunity to put his new knowledge to work. If the opportunity occurs, then he has to hope for some indication that his application of the ideas really worked. Without any feedback, he can never be completely sure that he understood the ideas fully in the first place, or that he applied them correctly, or that they were really valid and useful. These uncertainties leave the manager much more in the dark than seems necessary.

To remedy this, the Kepner-Tregoe programs attempt to

provide not only ideas but also practice in using them, and feedback on the results of the practice. All this is included in the same course format that appears to produce a significantly increased degree of learning on the part of the manager. These programs have been tested in a wide variety of situations within management, and by the end of 1964 some 15,000 managers had experienced this kind of intensive learning.

To be as specific as possible, we will here describe the APEX training program in which a group of fifteen or more managers grapples with the problems and decisions of the "APEX Company." This is a simulated organization made up of two divisions producing commercial and military products. The company is small enough to be readily understood by the managers assigned to it, and large enough to embody the kinds of business problems that face much bigger organizations. Its plan of organization is relatively clear-cut and provides both line and staff functions. It is a business setting within which problems are to be solved, but it is not a model of business. For here, unlike the management computer games, it is *not* the business itself which is of interest, but *the way in which the managers use the information* provided them in making their analyses of problems and their decisions. APEX is a framework in which managers can study and learn about the processes of business thought.

The managers receive in advance certain study materials to absorb on their own time before taking part in the daily problem sessions. These materials provide the concepts and procedures that will be used during the experiences of problem analysis and decision making. Each man also receives background information on the APEX Company, and ground rules covering each session. Managers meet both as a whole group and in separate groups of three or four or five men each throughout the five full days of the training.

The training sessions are usually held in a hotel or motel

where the managers live, eat, and work together from Monday morning through the following Friday afternoon. Each manager uses his own room as his office from which he communicates by phone to others on his team. When his team confers, they use one of the managers' rooms which has been equipped with a big paper pad and a tape recorder. The manager who leads each conference uses the paper pad to record data on each problem; the tape recorder registers the actual conversation of the managers during their conferences and this provides a direct feedback that they later use in studying the ways they worked on a problem together. But the main feedback occurs in the group sessions following each assignment when the leader explores with each team the procedures and reasoning they need in dealing with each assignment.

Daily sessions start at 8:30 A.M. and run through 5 P.M. or so, with an hour for lunch. The managers spend their evenings studying the tape-recorded sessions or the materials on the concepts and procedures, and work on those problem assignments that are to be done individually and reported on the next day. Frequently teams become so involved in solving a problem or making a decision, that they will work on into the early morning hours. But no cliques or special team combinations are allowed to develop; the managers are reassigned to new functions and to a new team on every one of the assignments given during the training program. Every manager has to learn how to work with every other manager during these team assignments, and his management function in APEX changes also from assignment to assignment.

Before each session, the managers and the course leader discuss the concepts and techniques involved, and the managers receive exercise materials setting out what has happened in the APEX Company recently in connection with some problem. The material includes memos from within their own departments, from other departments, or from outside the company. Also, policy directives, requests for information, financial statements, production and sales records, and other such information is given to the managers. Thus, the sales manager might have the latest sales forecast, a report on last week's finished product inventory from distribution, and cost estimates on a new product line for pricing purposes. A production manager may be told nothing about sales forecasts but would be given information on production scheduling, the latest quality control reports, manufacturing cost breakdowns, etc. The material varies with each of the management positions assumed by the participants during the week. Each of the members of the four or five man team is assigned to a different functional position each day. These positions include production manager, sales manager, distribution manager, financial manager, and industrial relations manager. There is also always a general manager and usually the post of executive vice president is assigned.

Each man first takes to his own "office" the material provided him on the APEX operations and on his own functional role. He reads through the information, organizes it, takes notes, or does what he would normally do in a similar real-life situation. He cannot expect to find a slip of paper neatly labeled, "This is a problem, solve here." Problems do not appear this way in real life or in the APEX Company. Most problems in real life appear first as seemingly unrelated bits of information that take on meaning as these pieces are put together. And this is the way problems appear to the members of each APEX management team. As the managers go through the materials, they begin to see their part in the various crises facing APEX, and they become aware of the actions these situations call for.

When the managers of a team have assimilated the information, they begin the task of managing APEX by getting together over the telephone or in conferences. They ask for or give information, set procedures, coordinate activities, give orders, make decisions, and do whatever else they feel is appropriate to the situation. Usually they get together promptly in conference, with each member of the team contributing his particular information on each particular problem. Because they have only about an hour and a half to arrive at an analysis and solution of these problems, they work under a real time pressure, which means they must coordinate their actions and communicate effectively. If they have a conference they have to use it well or lose valuable time. They must get the most out of the information they have available within the limited amount of time available if they are going to make the best decisions. They cannot have access to more information than is initially provided.

These controlled-experience situations are put together in such a way that the causes of the major problems confronting the APEX Company can be determined if the information available is used accurately and objectively. As in real life, if the decision is based on an inadequate analysis of a problem and its cause, the decision will be effective only through chance. If the decision is based on a good analysis, the managers have done all that was asked of them.

When the groups of managers have used up the time allotted for working with the exercise—whether or not they have solved their problems and made their decisions—they return to the conference room for a critical evaluation of their performances. In the critique, which is conducted by the course leader, the men probe into their own performance and that of the whole management team they were a part of. They examine the assumptions they have made and the ways in which they interpreted and used the information available to them. Some teams may find a problem's cause and solve it correctly, but getting the "right" answer to a particular problem is not the point at all. The emphasis is always on how efficiently they used the information they were given to arrive at the cause of the problem and make an appropriate decision. The feedback session aims to expose their own inadequate habits of thinking about problems and decisions and show them where they could have done much better had they followed the systematic procedures presented by the course leader.

Managers are very likely to find their first experience with the APEX exercise somewhat shattering. Having done their best in a difficult situation, using their full range of skills and ability, they are usually appalled at the uncritical questions they ask, and at their tendencies to jump to conclusions without examining all the information and to take action on problems before they know the cause. They find that their best, most valiant efforts usually end in an impasse when their approach to the information has not been rational. It is usually quite clear to them that they did not do the best job possible, and that they need to improve the way they have been managing.

From that point forward, they tend to become much more thoughtful in their approach to the management of APEX. They become more aware of the assumptions they make, of the procedures they use in arriving at the cause of a problem, and the decisions they may make about it. They begin, in short, to look more critically at their own methods. It is common to hear a manager wryly say, "Now I know why I have that trouble on the job," or "This is what I do all the time, but I never knew it before." The insights that managers gain in these critique sessions are among the most valuable products of the training program. With each succeeding exercise, they can apply these insights to their own procedures. Because they have the opportunity to keep on practicing what they are learning, they are more able to apply what they've learned back on their own jobs.

The course leader helps in the reconstruction of the problem analysis and decision making. He can provide feedback on information that was available but not used or inappropriately used, since he knows all of the facts of each case. He also has the advantage of having monitored the phone calls and the conferences intermittently while the teams were working on the problem. Thus he can spot behaviors that may have stood in the way of getting and using the information effectively. When the problems and most effective methods are reconstructed in a critique session, the managers have a yardstick against which they can compare their own use of the information and the approaches they took. They can assess what actually was done against what might have been and what should have been done.

This kind of training program makes great demands upon the capacities of the course leader. In effect, he has to become very quickly familiar with the differences between the managers and order his assignments to functions and to various teams accordingly. There can be nothing mechanical about the rotation of assignments and composition of teams if the full potential of the feedback is to be developed. We have therefore had to exercise great care in selecting not only the course leaders now on our staff, but also those leaders whom we train in companies that have been licensed to conduct the Kepner-Tregoe training programs.

Application and follow-up: However interesting a management development program may be, it must be of questionable worth if it does not provide for application that produces results on the job. The APEX program is by no means, therefore, limited to the presentation of new ideas and techniques for problem analysis and decision making. Because this program provides practice, it aims at the re-education of the thinking processes of managers who take part in it, so that when they get back on their jobs they will perform more efficiently with the information available to them. Because this training program makes the processes of problem analysis and decision making visible to the manager, it aims at getting him to think constantly of his job in the light of what he has learned. We want him to think, when a problem comes up, "Wait a minute. That's where I fell on my face in APEX. I better make sure I really test out the cause of this one." If he is going to avoid making uncritical assumptions and jumping to wrong actions he must consciously tell himself, when facing problems, "Recognize—separate—specify—find distinctions and changes—test causes."

Application of the ideas he has learned will not come about automatically back on the job. He will have to exert conscious self-discipline to avoid resuming his old behaviors. For this reason we present the one-week APEX course as the opening part of a six-month program of management development. Our experience over the last few years has shown that this is the best way to assure tangible, concrete results on the job.

The six-month program starts with the setting of objectives. What is it that the organization wants to get done in its management training? At this point we work with the client to formalize the criteria by which the program will be guided and its results assessed. We will help select the participants of a program, if the client wishes, and also prepare these managers for taking part in the program, sending them orientation and study materials well in advance. Their superiors are also informed as to the purpose and content of the program, and especially as to what they should expect in the way of applications on the job, and what they can do to maximize this.

During the one-week APEX course, the course leader is constantly looking for opportunities to show the participating managers how to apply the concepts and procedures to the kinds of problems they actually face on their jobs. A workbook containing special application study materials helps the manager survey his area of responsibility for points where he can apply what he is learning. As part of his evening assignments, each evening he explores another facet of problem analysis or decision making that has a bearing on his job. By the end of the five days of training he has a formal work plan for producing results with what he has learned.

Back on the job, the participating manager may or may not involve his superior in his plans for application. This will depend upon the superior's interest. But both will have been provided with a set of measures by which to assess the manager's progress, so that results can be made visible as they occur. Shortly after completing the APEX course, each participant receives a mailing from Kepner-Tregoe containing additional help and suggestions concerning applications. This material is based upon our experience as to the problems the participant will be running into at this stage of his learning. Shortly thereafter, his company may conduct a one and one-half day follow-up session, using the format, materials, and instructor's guide we provide. This session takes up problems encountered in making applications, analyzes both successes and failures, and reviews and sharpens up the manager's grasp of the basic concepts. Following this, he receives additional mailings at one-month intervals. The final mailing is primarily concerned with the measurement of what results have been achieved by each individual manager. Here again, his company and his superior, as well as the participant himself, are provided with criteria by which to assess what has been accomplished.

An overall assessment: No method of training and no body of concepts and procedures can guarantee results. There are no cure-alls in the development of managers, and old managers do not change into paragons of executive virtue overnight. For learning how to do any difficult task more efficiently is hard work. Furthermore, no matter how much effort is expended on learning, managers cannot carry away useful knowledge and increased skill from any experience unless it provides them with the three essentials of learning—new ideas, practice in using them, and feedback on the results. The approach we have described was designed as a way of combining these three essentials into a controlled experience for the improvement of problem analysis and decision making.

This approach has been more than ordinarily effective. Not all managers get results, and some very able managers simply do not use the ideas they have learned in the course. Or, if they do use them, they are not consciously aware of it and so are unlikely to apply the concepts and procedures systematically. But as the applications described in Chapter 9 demonstrate, results are produced by many managers, no matter what kind of activity they manage.

The ideas presented in this book and in the Kepner-Tregoe training programs are conceptual tools. As with any tools, they are made to be used, and that takes effort and self-discipline and concentration. As with any tools, a certain degree of skill must be developed before the tools feel easy to use. But once mastered, the ideas can never be forgotten. They become a way of managing that produces substantial continuing rewards. For the individual and for the organization, the application of these ideas means a better use of the resources and information at hand, and this in turn means that the expense of acquiring and mastering these tools is returned many times over.

Finally, the key to getting results through application is

planning that application and preparing for it. It cannot be assumed that application will happen after the concepts and procedures have been studied and practiced in the training program. For without planning and preparation for the application, good instruction has no lasting effect and results are almost accidental.

Annotated Bibliography

Note by the authors: There is much disagreement about problem solving and decision making. Different people use the words to mean different things and see these rooted in entirely different processes. The literature of problem solving and decision making reflects this disagreement; it is scattered and contradictory and includes a number of theories or lines of thought. We have presented our point of view in the preceding pages, and here we would like to provide a cross section of what some other workers in the field think. This bibliography is intended only as a sample; the list is not exhaustive or complete by any means. We have instead tried to pick out the best and most up-to-date source for each position or school of thought. Each reference gives a good starting point for the manager who wants to go into these matters somewhat further. The annotations are our own and represent our understanding of the viewpoints cited.

Abendroth, W. W. "The Research and Decision Making Process," in Jesse Shera *et al., Documentation in Action,* pp. 42–53 (New York: Reinhold, 1956).

> This article presents a unique view of problem analysis and decision making, describing the process as a form of calculus. Abendroth attempts to place the following steps into a mathematical-logic framework: (1) analysis of the decision area to discover applicable elements; (2)

establishment of the criteria for evaluation; (3) appraisal of known information and correction for bias; (4) isolation of unknown factors; (5) empirical values set upon known factors; (6) weighting of the pertinent elements as to relative importance; (7) projection of relative impacts on the objective, and synthesis into a course of action. Examples of these steps are given. Abendroth believes that the solving of problems and making of decisions, all of which he lumps together, can become a science if these seven systematic steps are followed. Interesting as an attempt to organize the process within the rules of calculus.

Benson, Bernard, S. "Let's Toss This Idea Up," *Fortune*, October, 1957.

A scathingly critical evaluation of brainstorming as a means of problem solving. Benson points out the dangers of having "potluck group-think" and "cerebral popcorn," as he terms it, take the place of systematic logic. He makes the point that novelty in itself is no guarantee of appropriateness. He also makes a needed distinction between solving a problem and deciding what to do next. An excellent rebuttal to the thesis of the creative problem-solving school.

Blake, Robert R., and Jane S. Mouton. *The Managerial Grid* (Houston: Gulf Publishing Co., 1964).

The authors hold that problems will be correctly solved and good decisions will be made if a culture or climate exists within the organization which allows free and objective use of information. It is therefore the manager's job to construct such a climate in which his subordinates have concern both for production and for people. The manager does this by example and training, through analysis of the work-team's performance as it deals with real-life problems. Blake and Mouton provide ideas relevant to good work-group operation, but not to problem solving per se, since it is their contention that efficient group operation is a prerequisite to solving any problem successfully. Their "managerial grid" is a way of representing simultaneous concern for production and for people, for measuring this in group performance, and for communicating information within the work-team. This is a practical, reality-oriented approach to group problem solving and is very much worth reading.

Bursk, Edward C., and John F. Chapman. *New Decision-making Tools for Managers* (Cambridge, Mass.: Harvard University Press, 1963).

Mathematical decision making is a new tool for managers. It deals with optimizing a large number of variables, solving problems dealing with uncertainty, and finding the relationships that apply between interesting factors. A major concern is how to collect and analyze data at minimum cost; another is how to relate objectives of a part to the overall objectives of the organization. But what is the problem? This is assumed by the authors to be apparent at the outset of the mathematical procedures. To the degree that it is apparent, mathematical approaches to decision making are correspondingly valuable. To the degree that analysis of the problem is obscured by the demands of mathematical nicety, violence is done to rationality, and the manager comes out on the short end of the stick. This book is the best source in its field, but it should be read with some skepticism: the world of the manager has not yet settled into mathematical quantifiability in all respects.

Conty, J. M. *Psychologie de la Decision* (Paris: Les Editions Organisation, 1959).

This book, soon to be translated into English, presents a means-ends analysis in the place of problem solving. Criteria of improvement or correction are set for the organization, for psychological variables of those involved, for superiors, and for the social climate or culture. Next, principles are derived that set the directions to be followed; then means of action are developed for carrying out the improvements stated. The choice between actions is made by balancing advantages against disadvantages. There is no determination of cause, or testing before action is taken. Conty assumes that the problem and its cause are both apparent and that only the choice of what to do about it remains. This is an excellent summary of the means-ends approach.

Cooper, Joseph D. *The Art of Decision Making* (Garden City, N.Y.: Doubleday, 1961).

This book is representative of the how-to-do-it approach. It provides no theory or rationale as to what problem solving and decision making are, but rather sets out a long list of maxims, rules, cautions, and guidelines. Cooper raises a number of good questions to be asked by the problem solver: Is the problem properly understood? Is the stated problem the real one? Does the problem "feel right"? Are you the right one to consider the problem? Do you have an open mind about it? Unfortunately the author provides neither answers nor the means of finding answers. This is an honest attempt to give guidance in a difficult area, but the lack of some unifying set of concepts degrades the whole effort to the cookbook level.

Drucker, Peter F. *Managing for Results* (New York: Harper & Row, 1964).

The job of the manager, according to Drucker, is not to solve problems and patch things up but rather to look for new opportunities and make decisions as to how these may best be used. He looks on problem solving— "which only restores normality"—as relatively nonrewarding. He sees the big gains as those coming from finding new alternatives and completely new ways of operating. He holds that looking into the future is the primary responsibility of a manager and that that is where the payoff lies. Implicit throughout this work is the assumption that the causes of failure are known and that opportunity is therefore recognizable. Given this assumption, Drucker's thesis makes a great deal of sense. But he does not deal explicitly with how to find the cause of a problem so that good decision making can proceed. This is a stimulating and thought-provoking book, well worth reading by any manager while holding Drucker's assumption critically in mind.

Gabriel, H. W. *Techniques of Creative Thinking for Management* (Englewood Cliffs, N.J.: Prentice-Hall, 1961).

This book is about problem solving by committee in the sheerest sense. Gabriel defines creative thinking as solving problems through use of the "multiple-mind technique." He describes this multiple-mind or committee approach as a "group of minds gathered together and caused to function simultaneously and collectively, but as parts of a unit mind instead of as independent minds." The committee acts to bring ideas to bear on problems and provides "prod devils" or leads to solutions which become "seed ideas." The function of the committee is then to grow final solutions from the seeds previously planted. Correcting the cause of a problem is considered by Gabriel to be "problem patching," and is to be avoided. He thinks the proper approach is to find an entirely new way of doing things whenever a problem arises. This is a superficial treatment of creativity and problem solving, typical of much that is accepted as efficient thought in this field of study.

Gordon, William J. J. *Synectics* (New York: Harper & Row, 1961).

Creative problem solving according to Gordon is the finding of a new alternative where the problem is the recognized need for a new way of doing things. To find a new alternative, one must look at the environment in a new way. This book stresses the psychological variables that allow an individual to see possibilities which were previously unseen by anyone. Gordon presents a highly systematized set of procedures and mechanisms which are fundamentally sound: detachment, or backing off from the situation; involvement, or projecting one's self into the situation; deferment, or thinking of principles and analogies rather than solutions; speculation, or fantasy and analogy beyond reality; autonomy of the object, or letting the problem dictate its own solution. The intent of these mechanisms is to make the person more flexible through systematic treatment of the problem solver rather than through systematic organization of the relevant information. Determination of cause and the testing of an explanation simply do not enter into this approach. This is an intriguing account of an approach that has enjoyed some measure of success and acceptance.

Gore, William J. *Administrative Decision-making: A Heuristic Model* (New York: Wiley, 1964).

Gore takes a position completely contrary to our own. He holds that there are two decision systems: the rational and the "heuristic." The rational is conscious, logical, and planned; it usually is applied to what is cut-and-dried and readily quantifiable. The heuristic system is held to be largely unconscious, intuitive, emotional, and unplanned, and it applies to the intangible and qualitative. According to Gore, most important management systems employ this heuristic system rather than the rational system. Though the adjective heuristic ordinarily describes a method that stimulates individual investigation, Gore's heuristic system is indeterminant to the degree that terms cannot be sharply defined, the finding of cause is neither possible nor useful, and the verification and testing of an explanation before taking action is unheard of and unnecessary. A problem is identified as the output of a "tension network" and is treated thereafter as a "stimulus to action." A decision in Gore's heuristic system is a consensus "arrived at through indigenous practices largely undisciplined by logic and untrammeled by scientific knowledge [with] a primitive quality." Rather than attempt to discipline and systematize the implicit and half-recognized factors entering into his heuristic system, Gore feels that one should accept this system as it is and define its steps. A complex model of the system is described with eighty-nine separate steps. Worth reading for a totally different point of view.

Jones, Manley H. *Executive Decision Making* (Homewood, Ill.: Richard D. Irwin, 1957).

This is one of the best books in the field: it attempts to set out what it is that a manager does in solving a problem. Jones is one of the few to treat problem solving as a separate topic. He sets out useful techniques and describes methods that are realistic and that meet the needs of a manager. Jones's major fault is that he wanders too far afield. Though he provides little theory or rationale behind the technique, he has produced a work from which most managers can gain good. He is one of the very few authors in this area who tries to approach problem solving and decision making from the position of the manager. His book is well worth reading as another view toward a systematic approach.

Jones, William D. *On Decision Making in Large Organizations* (Santa Monica, Calif.: RAND Corp., RM 3968 PR, 1964).

It is assumed in this work that all people in organizations are serious, dedicated, and able, and that they should be capable of solving problems correctly. Therefore, the author concludes that failure to solve prob-

lems must be the result of poor communications and a
lack of the relevant and important information. "The
observable weaknesses of organizational decision making," he states, "can be attributed to weaknesses in the
intra-organization communications process." To improve problem solving and decision making he says the
organization should be structured to provide enhanced
communications between decision makers. He reaches
the conclusion that automated data-processing systems
with centralized control will relieve much of the present
difficulty. This may be termed the dehumanized approach representative of a few computer addicts, and
it is worth the manager's attention as a sign of the
changing times.

Likert, Rensis, *New Patterns of Management* (New York: McGraw-
Hill, 1961).

This is probably the most extreme and most theoretical
statement of the position that good problem solving
and decision making is simply good group action. Likert
makes the basic, flat assumption that participative management is the best kind of management, and, therefore,
the task of management is to assure participation in all
respects. Group discussion, he holds, becomes the best
and only valid way to a good decision. In his view, problem solving is the coordinated gathering of data and the
integration of it in the group; decision making is the
selection of an action by acclamation. Accordingly, there
are no techniques of problem solving or decision making
per se, only better ways of working as group members.
Given Likert's assumption, these improved ways will, of
course, result in better decisions. His book is an interesting one for managers to sample, but they will find it difficult and far-removed from the practical reality they
must contend with day by day. Recommended for the
studious and very patient.

Maier, Norman F. *Problem-solving Discussions and Conferences* (New York: McGraw-Hill, 1963).

Almost all management problems are solved through some use of the conference, according to Maier, and he concentrates on leadership of the problem-solving discussion or conference as the key variable of success. He gives two dimensions of an effective decision: its quality, or ultimate rightness, and its acceptance by those who must implement it. So problems are to be identified at the outset as those which must be of high quality, and those which must have full acceptance. No matter how correct it may be, a decision becomes useless if it is not accepted, and the way to gain acceptance is to solve the problem through group discussion. The more skillful the conference leader, the more successful the conference, and, incidentally, the higher the quality of the solution will be. Maier's solving process starts with "locating the problem" or deciding what needs to be done. Cause, however, is not determined. The statement of the problem includes the current situation plus the objectives to be obtained. Moderate attention is given to getting out the real facts of a problem: "It is clear that solutions based upon the facts that are known have a better chance of succeeding than those that have a lesser basis of reality." But Maier thinks that the best solution is the one that most subscribe to on a voting basis, essentially, regardless of its truth or objective correctness. This book gives an excellent treatment of conference leadership as a necessary management skill, whether or not one agrees with the problem solving theory that is implied.

Osborn, Alex F. *Applied Imagination* (New York: Scribner, 1953). This is the basic text on brainstorming, the idea from which all creative problem solving has sprung. Osborn, an original partner in the advertising firm of Batten,

Barton, Durstine & Osborn, describes the advantages of brainstorming and how it can be used. The technique is nonanalytic and is simply a search for new alternatives. While not stated in so many words, the brainstorming credo is to solve problems by taking new action. The aim is to generate as many ideas for action as possible, on the assumption that out of many there will be found the few that are relevant and valuable. Brainstorming, or "applied imagination," is valuable as a means of uncovering information, but its worth as a problem-solving method is open to serious question. Osborn's book is one of the classics in its field.

Simon, Herbert A. *The New Science of Management Decision* (New York: Harper & Row, 1960).

This is the best statement of problem-solving theory to be found in the literature on the subject. Simon has spent years attempting to simulate on the computer the workings of the human mind. As a result of his research, he has independently come up with two of our basic concepts: that a problem is a deviation from some standard, and that the cause of a problem is an unplanned and unanticipated change. Simon has gone on further to consider the role of the computer in management activity and in the making of decisions. All that he has discovered as fundamental to thinking within the framework of his computer researches may be generalized to individual problem solving. This is because, in the treatment of information, both individual and computer make use of the same basic mechanism, the method of comparisons. Man and computer compare should against actual to identify problems, and compare IS against IS NOT to identify unique or distinctive factors. We feel that Simon, using another route, has come very close to what we hold to be the truth. His book is required reading for managers seriously interested in the field of problem solving and decision making.

Index

SET CONTINGENCY
ACTIONS

- Minimize
  Problem Effects

SET CONTROLS

- Trigger Contingency Actions
- Progress vs. Plan

TAKE PREVENTIVE ACTION

- Remove Cause

ANTICIPATE POSSIBLE
CAUSES

- Assess Probabilities

DIRECTION AND
CONTROL

ACTION
CALLED
FOR

YO

SIT

SEPARATE, SET PRIORITY

- Probability
- Seriousness
- Invisibility

POTENTIAL PROBLEM
ANALYSIS

ANTICIPATE POTENTIAL
PROBLEMS

Should
± Could

Potential Deviation

PLAN AND
FORESIGHT
REQUIRED

DECISION MADE

ASSESS ADVERSE
CONSEQUENCES

- Minimize Threat

COMPARE AND CHOOS

MUSTS: GO/NO GO

WANTS: Relative fit